Corporate Acquisitions and Mergers in Indonesia

Corporate Acquisitions and Mergers in Indonesia

Third Edition

Idwan Ganie
Arum Tarina

Lubis Ganie Surowidjojo Law Firm

This book was originally published as a chapter in Corporate Acquisitions and Mergers.

General Editor: Peter Begg

Wolters Kluwer

Published by:
Kluwer Law International B.V.
PO Box 316
2400 AH Alphen aan den Rijn
The Netherlands
E-mail: international-sales@wolterskluwer.com
Website: lrus.wolterskluwer.com

Sold and distributed by:
Wolters Kluwer Legal & Regulatory U.S.
7201 McKinney Circle
Frederick, MD 21704
United States of America
Email: customer.service@wolterskluwer.com

ISBN 978-94-035-3360-5

e-Book: ISBN 978-94-035-3361-2
web-PDF: ISBN 978-94-035-3362-9

Contents

Lubis Ganie Surowidjojo Law Firm

Lubis Ganie Surowidjojo Law Firm (LGS) was established in 1985, and for more than thirty years we have been one of the largest and most respected law firms in the country. We have secured our position as the premier Indonesian corporate transaction and commercial litigation law firm. We have over a hundred lawyers with experience representing a diverse range of clients, including domestic and multinational corporations, public and private companies, Government instrumentalities, and state-owned enterprises. We work closely with our clients to understand their problems, determine their needs, and arrive at practical solutions that are both cost effective and viable over the long term.

We strive to understand a client's needs and the legal complexities faced by them in Indonesia's highly dynamic legal and business landscape, translate this into a solution, and then see the successful outcome. To this end, we approach our clients' assignments with a pragmatic view that is driven by a deep understanding of their business needs and of the surrounding practicalities of the legal and business landscape that they operate in.

Representative Clients

Goldman Sachs; Hitachi; Hutchison (Hong Kong); Medco Energi International; Ministry of Finance of the Republic of Indonesia; Mitsui & Co., Ltd; Sime Darby (Malaysia); Temasek Holdings (Private) Limited

Practice Areas

- Commercial Transaction & Commercial Disputes

Contact Details

Dr Mohamed Idwan ('Kiki') Ganie, S.H., FSIArb.

Lubis Ganie Surowidjojo

Menara Imperium 30th Floor

Jl. H. R. Rasuna Said Kav. 1 Kuningan

Jakarta 12980, Indonesia

Tel.: +62 21 831-5005, 831-5025

Fax: +62 21 831-5015, 831-5018

E-mail: ganie@lgslaw.co.id

Website: www.lgsonline.com

Authors

Dr M. Idwan Ganie, SH ('Kiki') Ganie is a Founding Partner of Lubis Ganie Surowidjojo. He graduated from the Faculty of Law at the University of Indonesia and holds a PhD in Law from the University of Hamburg. Dr Ganie has completed further studies at the Institute for Advanced Legal Studies in London; the Max Planck Institute for International Private Law in Hamburg, Germany; and in political studies at the *Staatswissenschaftliche Fakultaet* of the University of Zurich. He is a licensed Indonesian capital market lawyer and a member of the Asia Pacific Bar Association.

Dr Ganie has more than forty years of legal experience and specializes in commercial transactions and commercial litigation, including alternative dispute resolution and has acted as an expert in several court and arbitration proceedings. His expertise covers general corporate/company law, banking law, finance (including lease finance), mining, investment, acquisitions, infrastructure projects/project finance, antitrust, and shipping/aviation, with a particular focus on corporate governance and compliance.

His international commercial transaction and litigation clients include Goldman Sachs (US), Temasek Holdings (Singapore), Hutchison Whampoa (Hong Kong), Mitsui (Japan) and Hitachi.

He is a senior lecturer of the Faculty of Law at the University of Indonesia, a lecturer for the Indonesian Bar Association (PERADI), and a frequent speaker at international conferences and seminars covering a range of Indonesian legal issues. His publications include works on such topics as mining, shipping, finance, and dispute settlement.

Dr Ganie is a chairman of the Association of Indonesian Antitrust Lawyers, President of the Indonesian Court of Arbitration for Sports, a member of the regional panel of the Singapore International Arbitration Centre (SIAC) and AIAC (formerly KLRCA) in Kuala Lumpur, a fellow (FSIarb) of the Singapore Institute of Arbitrators, sports arbitrator with CAS in Lausanne, and a member of the Association for International Arbitration (AIA). In 2017, Asian Legal Business (ALB) named Dr Ganie Indonesia's Managing Partner of the Year. In 2020 he was named Commended External Counsel of the Year voted entirely by in-house counsels throughout Asia, Africa and the Middle East and, most recently, two different international publications in the legal profession have named Dr Ganie Indonesia's Arbitration and Litigation Lawyer/Advisor of the Year. He speaks Indonesian, English and German, and understands Dutch.

Ms Arum Tarina, SH, LLM is a Lawyer at Lubis Ganie Surowidjojo. She graduated from the Faculty of Law, University of Indonesia, majoring in Business Law. During her university studies, she received honours as a Leading Student in National Human Rights and Corruption Moot Court Competition for three consecutive years. Before joining Lubis Ganie Surowidjojo, she has worked in-house and with another Jakarta-based law firm. She holds a license as an advocate from Peradi. She is a lecturer of the Study Program of Law at the Pelita Bangsa University, Indonesia. Her practice includes competition law, technology law, investment law, corporate law, and commercial litigation. In 2012 she concluded her studies at Tilburg University, the Netherlands, earning a Master of Laws (LLM) in Law and Technology. She speaks Indonesian and English.

List of Abbreviations

AoA	Articles of Association
AGMS	Annual General Meeting of Shareholders
AMDAL	*Analisis Dampak Lingkungan (*Environmental Impact Analysis)
APBN	*Anggaran Pendapatan dan Belanja Negara* (State Budget)
BEPS	Base Erosion and Profit Shifting
BI	Bank of Indonesia
BKPM	*Badan Koordinasi Penanaman Modal* (Indonesia Investment Coordinating Board)
BoC	Boards of Commissioners
BoD	Boards of Directors
CbCR	Country-by-Country Reporting
CITR	Corporate Income Tax Return
DER	Debt to Equity Ratio
DGT	Directorate General of Tax
DKP-TKA	*Dana Kompensasi Penggunaan Tenaga Kerja Asing* (Compensation Funds of Utilization of Foreign Worker)
DNI	*Daftar Negatif Investasi* (Negative Investment List)
FCPA	US Foreign Corrupt Practices Act
FDI	Foreign Direct Investment
GoI	Government of the Republic of Indonesia
IASB	International Accounting Standard Board

GMS	General Meeting of Shareholder
IFRS	International Financial Reporting Standards
KBLI	*Klasifikasi Baku Lapangan Usaha Indonesia* (Indonesia Standard Industrial Classification)
KPPU	*Komisi Pengawas Persaingan Usaha* (The Indonesian Business Competition Supervisory Commission)
LKPM	*Laporan Kegiatan Penanaman Modal* (Capital Investment Activity Report)
LKTP	*Laporan Keuangan Tahunan Perusahaan* (Audited Annual Financial Statements)
MoLHR	Ministry of Law and Human Rights
MPR	*Majelis Permusyawaratan Rakyat* (People's Representative Council)
NIB	*Nomor Induk Berusaha* (Business Identification Number)
NPWP	*Nomor Pokok Wajib Pajak* (Taxpayer Identification Number)
OJK	*Otoritas Jasa Keuangan* (Financial Services Authority)
OSS	Online Single Submission
P3B	*Persetujuan Penghindaran Pajak Berganda* (Avoidance of Double Taxation Agreement)
PE	Permanent Establishment
PKP	*Pengusaha Kena Pajak* (VATable Entrepreneurs)
PMA	*Penanaman Modal Asing* (Foreign Capital Investment)

PMDN	*Penanaman Modal Dalam Negeri* (Domestic Capital Investment)
PSAK	*Pernyataan Standar Akuntansi Keuangan* (Indonesian Financial Accounting Standards)
PT	*Perseroan Terbatas* (Limited Liability Company)
PT PMA	*Perseroan Terbatas Penanaman Modal Asing* (Limited Liability Company with Foreign Ownership)
RAPBN	*Rancangan Anggaran Pendapatan Belanja Negara* (State Budget Plan)
RPTKA	*Rencana Penggunaan Tenaga Kerja Asing* (Foreign Worker Recruitment Plan)
SOEs	State-Owned Enterprises
VAT	Value Added Tax
WLFK	*Wajib Lapor Fasilitas Kesejahteraan* (Manpower Welfare Facility Report)
WLTK	*Wajib Lapor Tenaga Kerja* (Manpower Report)

Important Links

The Ministry of Law and Human Rights	www.ahu.go.id
The Indonesia Stock Exchange	www.idx.co.id
The Indonesia Investment Coordinating Board	www.bkpm.go.id
The Indonesian Business Competition Supervisory Commission	www.kppu.go.id
The Online Single Submission	www.oss.go.id
The Directorate General of Tax	www.pajak.go.id
The Supreme Court	www.mahkamahagung-.go.id
The Financial Service Authority	www.ojk.go.id
The Ministry of Manpower	www.kemnaker.go.id

1 LOCAL ECONOMIC, POLITICAL, AND CULTURAL ASPECTS

1.1 Country Profile

1.1.1 Geographical Location

[01] Indonesia is located in Southeast Asia, lying between the Indian Ocean and the Pacific Ocean. It is located in a strategic location connecting East Asia, South Asia, and Oceania.

[02] Indonesia's borders include land and maritime borders with Malaysia, Papua New Guinea, and Timor Leste, as well as shared maritime boundaries with Australia, India, Palau, Philippines, Singapore, Thailand and Vietnam. The capital city is Jakarta. However, Indonesia's president, Joko Widodo, has announced that the national capital will move from Jakarta, on the island of Java, to the province of East Kalimantan, on the island of Borneo by 2024 at the earliest.

[03] Indonesia is the world's largest island country and the 14th-largest country by land area, with 1 904 569 square kilometres (735 358 square miles), including 93 000 square kilometres (35 908 square miles) of inland seas (straits, bays, and other bodies of water).

[04] Indonesia's geography, in close proximity to the equator, results in a tropical climate across the archipelago with relatively even year-round temperatures. Also, Indonesia has good conditions for tourism, especially focusing on its tropical destinations, with white sand beaches, blue sky, and cultural attractions. Beach resorts and hotels have been developed in some of the popular tourist destinations, especially with Bali island as the primary destination.

1.1.2 Population and Population Growth

[05] Indonesia has a population of about 273m, which represents a 3.51% share of the global aggregate, and is the 4th most populous country in the world. Beyond that, Indonesia is predicted to benefit from a significant 'demographic bonus' or 'demographic dividend' (a condition in which the productive age population is more than the non-productive population) in 2020–2030, as a result of robust economic growth when the total dependency ratio will be at an all-time low. This is expected to reach 70% of the total population by 2030.

[06] Most of the population lives on the island of Java, the world's most populous island. Jakarta is currently Indonesia's capital, the centre of its economy, cultural politics and the most populated city in the country with a population which is estimated at 10 770 487 as of 2020.

1.1.3 Language

[07] The country's official and national language is Indonesian. Most Indonesians also speak at least one of more than seven-hundred local languages, often as their first language. Javanese is the most widely spoken. The most common foreign language in Indonesia is English. However, communication with authorities must take place in Bahasa Indonesia.

[08] The government of Indonesia issued Law No. 24 of 2009 on the State Flag, Language and Coat of Arms, as well as National Anthem *juncto* Presidential Regulation No. 63 of 2019 on the Use of Bahasa Indonesia, which might have a significant impact on the negotiation, drafting, and execution of Indonesian contracts (namely, any contract involving Indonesian parties) among others: a contract with foreign parties cannot explicitly state that the contract is exclusively or predominantly negotiated in a foreign language, and the Bahasa Indonesia version of any contract involving Indonesian entities must be executed on the same day as the signing of the non-Indonesian or English version, as opposed to having the parties agree on a certain future date to have the contract translated into Bahasa Indonesia.

1.1.4 Currency

[09] The rupiah (Rp) is the official currency of Indonesia. Issued and controlled by Bank Indonesia (BI), the ISO 4217 currency code for the Indonesian rupiah is IDR.

[10] As of 31 March 2015, BI issued Regulation No. 17/3/PBI/2015 on the Mandatory Use of Rupiah within Indonesian Territory. It was issued as part of BI's strategy to strengthen the rupiah's exchange rate and to implement Law No. 7 of 2011 on Currency, which mandates that all transactions taking place within Indonesia, both cash and non-cash, should use rupiah. However, the 2015 Regulation excludes ten transactions from the obligation to use rupiah, namely:

(1) certain transactions for implementing the State Budget (*Anggaran Pendapatan* dan *Belanja Negara* – APBN);
(2) acceptance or disbursement of a grant from or to overseas;
(3) international transactions;
(4) bank saving in the form of foreign exchange;
(5) international financing transactions;
(6) foreign exchange activities performed by banks;
(7) transactions in securities that are issued by the government in the primary and secondary market;
(8) other transactions in foreign exchange under prevailing laws and regulations;
(9) transactions by money changers; and
(10) carriage of foreign banknotes to or from Indonesia under prevailing laws and regulations.

1.1.5 Natural Resources

[11] Indonesia is endowed with an abundance of natural resources like oil and natural gas, coal, tin, copper, gold and nickel, while agriculture products include rice, palm oil, tea, coffee, cacao, medicinal plants, spices and rubber. Renewable resources include biomass energy (such as ethanol), hydropower, geothermal power, wind energy and solar energy.

1.1.6 Employment Cost and Availability of Labour

[12] The main components of employment cost are the employee's salary, taxes and social security contributions. Wages in Indonesia range from IDR3 070 000 (approximately USD210) per month (minimum wage) to IDR54 200 000 (approximately USD680) per month (maximum average wage, although the actual maximum is higher). As the minimum wage differs for every province and region/ municipal, and are usually determined once per calendar year, foreign investors should seek help from registered local advisors. The median wage in Indonesia is around IDR11 400 000 (approximately USD780) per month, which is significantly low. There are regions where people are willing to work for salaries which are below the average, and this makes such places attractive for manufacturing and production facilities. The new regulation set about salaries for part time employees that can be paid by the hour, by the enactment of the Government Regulation No. 36 of 2021 on Wages.

[13] The number of individuals in the workforce in February 2020 was 137.91m, up by 1.73m compared to February 2019. In contrast to this increase in the available workforce, the Labor Force Participation Rate fell by 0.15 percentage points, as the unemployment rate in February 2020 was 4.99%. However, due to the COVID-19 pandemic, the unemployment rate in Indonesia is expected to be 8.50% according to Trading Economics global macro models and analysts' expectations. In the long-term, the unemployment rate in Indonesia is anticipated to trend around 8.50% in 2021 and 7.50% in 2022, according to Trading Economics' econometric models.

[14] In 2019, the literacy rate among Indonesians between the ages of 15 and 19 was 99.79%. For 20–24 years old, it was 99.74%, for 25–29 years old 99.53%, for 30–34 years old 99.18%, for 35–39 years old 98.75%, for 40–44 years old 98.31%, for 45–49 years old 97.64%, and for those over 50 years old it was 87.58%. Nowadays, it is common for young people to pursue higher education in Indonesia.

1.1.7 Physical Infrastructure: Road, Rail Links, Ease of Travel

[15] Another challenge for a huge archipelago such as Indonesia is the provision of infrastructure to support economic activities. Connectivity between regions should be developed to accelerate and expand economic development. The provision of infrastructure which encourages connectivity will reduce transportation and

logistics costs thereby improving product competitiveness and accelerating economic growth.

[16] In the 2020 state budget plan (RAPBN), the budget was increased by 4.9% from the 2019 infrastructure budget allocation which is IDR399.7 trillion (approximately USD27bn), and the element of the infrastructure budget that rises most steeply is road construction. In addition, according to the Minister of Public Works and Public Housing, the programme that will continue to be carried out during the pandemic is the construction of toll roads, because the improvement of conditions for road and railroad transportation is one of the government's top priorities.

1.2 Government and Political System

1.2.1 General Political Environment

[17] Indonesia is a large and widely spread archipelagic state whose population and the majority of whose development is generally concentrated on Java island. However, natural resources in Sumatra, Kalimantan (Borneo), and Papua are playing an increasingly important role in the Indonesian economy and politics. In this respect, there has been a certain degree of 'resource nationalism', which has at times resulted in what could be viewed as protectionist policies towards the natural resource sector. At the same time, the government fully realizes that the outlying islands severely lack much-needed infrastructure, and that such development is often only possible through foreign investment.

[18] Indonesia is generally a politically stable country and has a presidential system of democracy. Having maintained political stability, Indonesia is one of East Asia Pacific's most vibrant democracies, emerging as a confident middle-income country.

[19] Indonesia applies the *Trias Politica* that recognizes the separation of the legislative, executive and judicial branches of government. The executive institution is centralized under the president, the vice president and the cabinet of ministers. The cabinet is a presidential cabinet in which the ministers report to the president and do not represent political parties. Since 2004, the president and vice president have been directly elected for a five-year term, following which the president can be re-elected for only one more term.

[20] The legislative authority is under the People's Consultative Assembly (MPR). This consists of two bodies, namely the Parliament, composed of members of political parties, and the Regional Representative Council (DPD) comprising representatives from each province in Indonesia. Following the Amendment of the 1945 Constitution, the membership of the MPR (starting from the period 1999 to 2004) was amended to include not only members of the parliament (DPR) but also members of the DPD. The parliament members and the DPD members are elected every five years.

[21] The Judicial system is independent and has the power to organize the judicature to enforce law and justice. The Judiciary of Indonesia comprises the Supreme Court of Indonesia and the Constitutional Court of Indonesia together with public courts, religious courts, administrative courts and military courts.

1.2.2 Environment for Investors and Entrepreneurs

[22] Indonesia's economy is on the rise. The country is taking its place as a major destination for foreign investment and entrepreneurship. Indonesia's economy is generally based on free-market principles, but major constraints remain. First, protectionist policies (mostly measures to increase old or impose new tariffs and to regulate import and export quotas) continue to be a popular economic and political instrument of Indonesian governments.

[23] Based on the Global Entrepreneurship Index Rank of All Countries in 2019, Indonesia is ranked 75th in the world out of 137 countries. The Indonesian government has been trying to encourage entrepreneurship development by supporting the development of small and medium enterprises in the country, since these enterprises provide an avenue for the testing and development of entrepreneurial ability.

[24] During the past few years, there has been an improvement in the entrepreneurial environment and an increase in start-up initiatives, especially in the IT sector. Indonesia already has four 'unicorns' (Tokopedia, Bukalapak, Go-Jek, and Traveloka), and it is the country with the most unicorns in Southeast Asia, competing head-to-head with Singapore. At the moment, Indonesia has nearly 147m internet users (55% of its total population). This booming digital growth lays the foundations for Indonesia to reap significant economic benefits.

[25] For investors and start-ups, many of the most successful players are foreign entities, which explain why the government is keen to draw help from all quarters, and the authorities are taking steps to ensure clear regulatory requirements to boost the confidence of the players.

1.2.3 Interlinking with Global Financial and Trade System

[26] Indonesia is a member of several important international financial and trade organizations, such as the Association of South-East Asian Nations (ASEAN), the Asia-Pacific Economic Cooperation (APEC), the World Trade Organization (WTO), the International Monetary Fund (IMF), and the World Bank. In addition, Indonesia is the only representative country for Southeast Asia in the G20 (Group of Twenty).

1.3 Legal System

1.3.1 Indonesian Legal System

[27] Indonesia has a civil law legal system. It was inherited from the Dutch and adopted at the time of Indonesia's independence. Dutch civil law is derived from the French 'Code Civil' and the latter is historically and conceptually derived from Roman law. The Dutch colonial occupation left a legacy of Dutch colonial law, which continues in the Indonesian Civil Code, the Indonesian Commercial Code and the Indonesian Criminal Code. Following Indonesia's independence in 1945, the country started to establish its own modern Indonesian law, modifying existing Dutch legal principles and drawing from the customary law (*adat*) that existed before Dutch colonization, as well as Islamic law (sharia) which applies to Muslims.

[28] Indonesian legislation comes in different forms. The official hierarchy of Indonesian legislation (from top to bottom), according to Law No. 12 of 2011 as amended by Law No. 15 of 2019 concerning Law Making, is as follows:

(1) 1945 Constitution (*Undang-Undang Dasar* 1945 or UUD'45).
(2) Resolutions of the People's Representative Council (MPR) (*Ketetapan Majelis Permusyawaratan Rakyat*, Tap MPR).
(3) Law and Government Regulation in Lieu of Law.
(4) Government Regulation.
(5) Presidential Regulation.
(6) Provincial Regulation.
(7) Regency/Municipal Regulation.

1.3.2 Law Enforcement

[29] Indonesia boasts increasingly free economic development supported by modern company law, capital market law, bank and banking systems, financial services,[1] fair competition law, tax law, and laws particular to certain industries. These industries include oil and gas, mining, electricity, infrastructure development, shipping, civil aviation, clean water, etc. The modern laws referred to above were drafted to be compatible with the laws recognized in developed countries, to the extent those laws are compatible with the provisions and spirit of the Indonesian Constitution and national interests. In the absence of prevailing legislation to the contrary, the concept of freedom of contract is adopted and is widely accepted to serve the business interests of business players. According to World Bank data in May 2019, the average time required to enforce a contract in Indonesia is 403 days, and Indonesia Ranks 139 out of 190 countries in terms of enforcement of contracts.

[30] Indonesia has a vibrant democracy and a reasonably developed legal system. An issue that has unfortunately persisted for some decades in Indonesia is the level of corruption, which generally affects government officials and courts, particularly

[1] The World Bank. Doing Business 2020. Washington D.C.: World Bank, 2020, p. 4

those at first and second instance. In addition court proceedings can take a significant amount of time to reach a final resolution. This is in spite of the fact that the Supreme Court already establishes a guideline whereby the first instance (district court) should take a maximum of 5 months, the second instance (High Court) a maximum of 3 months, and the third instance (Supreme Court) a maximum of 250 days.

[31] With effect from January 2020, Indonesia has made the enforcement of contracts easier by introducing an electronic case management system for judges called '**e-court**' (which includes online case registration, online court fee payment, and online summonses to the parties) as well as '**e-litigation**' (online proceedings). However notwithstanding these convenient new developments, foreign judgments are not enforceable in Indonesia, as Indonesia is not a party to any international agreements or conventions on the enforcement of foreign judgments. Enforcement requires the commencement of new proceedings, with the foreign judgment or decision used as evidence.

[32] Furthermore, Indonesia has made the identification of acquisition targets easier by enabling searches through the Ministry of Law and Human Rights of the Republic of Indonesia (MoLHR). This uses an internet online system called '**AHU-Online**' (http://www.ahu.go.id) where much information is provided, including detailed information (i.e., full name, place and date of birth, occupation, address and nationality) relating to the shareholders, board members, and members of the board commissioners of individual companies. Access to the Companies List and Database is open to the public, provided that they are granted a company profile, and to law enforcement authorities.

1.4 Current Economic Aspects

1.4.1 Growth Rates of the Economy

[33] Indonesia is a growing powerhouse in Southeast Asia. A member of the G20, Indonesia's GDP in 2019 showed a growth rate of 5% and stood at USD1trillion, the largest in the region. It is touted by analysts to be among the new economies to watch out for. Indonesia is part of the newly coined acronym 'MIST' (Mexico, Indonesia, South Korea, and Turkey) owing to its potential as an emerging market.

[34] However, the combination of the trade war between the US and China, the COVID-19 pandemic, and the oil price war at the beginning of 2020 resulted in a tense and heavily challenging year for the world's community. The COVID-19 pandemic will continue to have adverse implications for the world and for Indonesia's economy this year. The World Bank is projecting Indonesia's economic growth this year to remain depressed at 2.1%. This is due to the continued widespread distribution of COVID-19 both domestically and abroad. BI has also revised the projected economic growth of Indonesia to remain below 5% or only around 2.5%. Although the relationship between economic growth and inflation is one of the debatable issues, the Central Statistics Agency recorded an inflation of only 0.98%

(year-to-date) or 1.54% inflation (year-on-year) due to a 0.10% deflation at the end of July 2020, the weakest in the past two decades. The main contributor to the drop in prices was the food, drinks, and tobacco category of expenses, followed by the transportation sector. Nevertheless the Government remains optimistic that the Indonesian economy will grow in 2021 in spite of the COVID-19 pandemic.

1.4.2 M&A Trends

[35] The Indonesian Business Competition Supervisory Commission (KPPU)'s website registered 90 M&A deals in 2019 and 104 M&A deals in 2020 (including both share and assets acquisitions) meeting the threshold for merger notification to the KPPU. Private M&A transactions still dominate the market (as confirmed by public data from the KPPU). Among other reasons for this is that the complex regulatory framework and procedures for M&A involving public companies often lead to lengthier deal times and costlier transactions. The past year has seen a significant increase in the number of foreign companies pursuing investment in local companies, especially in the technology and finance sectors.

[36] In addition, based on figures from the Indonesia Investment Coordinating Board (BKPM) regarding investment realization, including foreign direct investment realization, investments in the first and second quarters (January–June 2020) reached USD3 583.2m, dropping 9.2% year-on-year in the first quarter and 6.9% year-on-year in the second quarter. It was feared that the COVID-19 pandemic and a new financial crisis would adversely impact M&A activity in Indonesia. However, the government has been stepping up efforts to attract new investment both from local and foreign companies – among other measures by developing a 4 000-hectare industrial park in Batang Regency, Central Java.

1.5 Main Industries

1.5.1 Key Sectors

[37] Indonesia's main sectors, in terms of employment and value added, include the service sector (financial institutions, transportation and communications), the industrial sector (manufacturing of textiles, cement, chemical fertilizers, electronic products, rubber tyres, clothing and shoes, and wood processing), and the agricultural sector (rubber, rice, sugarcane, coffee, tea, tobacco, palm oil, coconuts and spices), as broken down below:

Economic Activity by Sector	*Industry*	*Services*	*Agriculture*
Employment (in % of Total Employment)	22.0	47.8	30.3

Economic Activity by Sector	*Industry*	*Services*	*Agriculture*
Value Added (in % of GDP)	39.7	43.6	12.8
Value Added (Annual % Change)	4.3	5.6	3.9

Source: Latest available data from World Bank.

[38] The top five leading sectors, involving the largest investment in the first quarter of 2020, are listed below:

(1) Transportation, Warehousing, and Telecommunications
(2) Basic Metal, Metal-Based Goods, Non-Machinery and Equipment Industry
(3) Electricity, Gas, and Water Supply
(4) Housing, Industrial Estate, and Office Building
(5) Food Crops, Plantation, and Livestock.

1.5.2 Foreign Investment

[39] The GoI exercises control over foreign investment under the supervision of the Capital Investment Coordinating Board (BKPM). Exemptions apply to financial services (banks, insurance companies, securities companies and the like), the foreign investment supervision of which is under the Financial Services Authority (OJK), as well as to oil companies, the supervision of which is under the Special Task Force for Upstream Oil and Gas Business Activities and the Ministry of Energy and Mineral Resources.

[40] Previously the GoI also controls foreign investment through what is known as the negative investment list or DNI, which is outlined in Presidential Regulation No. 44 of 2016 on the List of Business Fields That Are Closed and Business Fields That Are Conditionally Open for Investment. However, as the GoI is aiming to bring positive image for inviting more opportunities for foreign investors, the negative investment list is now replaced by the 'Positive Investment List' through the issuance of Presidential Regulation No. 10 of 2021 on Investment Business Activities ('PR No. 10/2021') on 2 February 2021, and it will take effect in March 2021. PR No. 10/2021 significantly reduces the amount of businesses that are subject to certain foreign ownership restrictions and it simplifies the investment list.

1.5.3 The Role of the State in the Economy

[41] In Indonesia, the state plays an important role, including administering prices for some basic goods such as fuel, rice and electricity. Also through the state-owned enterprises (SOEs), which play a crucial role in the economy, as many of them have important public policy objectives. This is because the Constitution of the Republic of Indonesia of 1945, Article 33 paragraph (2) provides that 'production sectors that are vital to the state and that affect the livelihood of a considerable part of the population are to be controlled by the state.' And paragraph (3) stipulates that: 'The land and the waters, as well as the natural riches therein, are to be controlled by the state to be exploited to the greatest benefit of the people.' Other than the sectors mentioned above, markets are generally left to private enterprises.

[42] International corporate, project and structured financing activities are pretty much supported by prevailing regulations. However, increasingly complex transactions are to be expected when the State, State-owned or local government-owned enterprises are involved as parties or as direct stakeholders in the transaction. In provincial Indonesia, local regulations, social conditions, religious, cultural and customary issues all have to be taken into account. LGS partners and lawyers have vast experience in this respect and are well-equipped to assist the government, investors, lenders, business leaders and their supporting professionals in identifying relevant legal issues, fact finding and recommending practical and acceptable solutions for all parties – particularly in highly complex corporate, project and structured finance, through many available structures including corporate financing, equity and debt financing, project-related financing, debt restructuring and refinancing and their hybrid products.

1.6 Cultural Aspects

1.6.1 Investment Climate

[43] Indonesia is generally open and welcoming to foreign investment. While Indonesia is ranked 73 out of 190 in the World Bank's annual Ease of Doing Business Index 2020, and ranked 50 out of 141 countries in the World Economic Forum's Global Competitiveness Report 2019, the government's target for Indonesia is to improve these rankings every year. In particular, one of the government's priorities in the economic sector is to improve the ranking of the Ease of Doing Business Index, with the overall aim of increasing foreign investment.

[44] Indonesian legislation differentiates between local and foreign investors in terms of authorized capital. For foreign investors this is more expensive. However, Indonesia can be considered a relatively cheap place for doing business. Labour costs are not high, and Indonesia is considered a good place to outsource services and business process. Indonesia is in 4th place out of 50 countries in 2019's Global Services Location Index which is based on corporate input, current remote services activity, and government initiatives to promote the sector. Indonesia is regarded as showing major improvement in the political environment, helping to offset minor declines in both financial attractiveness and people skills and availability. Indonesia's proximity to Australia makes business process outsourcing (BPO) services especially attractive to companies there.

[45] Generally speaking, the higher the risks, the higher the potential yields, and investing always encompasses risk. Investing in Indonesia can be highly worthwhile. However, it also entails more risk than investing in a developed country, because Indonesia contains a number of country-specific dynamics and characteristics which can disturb investment and challenge a climate conducive to investment and business. Among other challenges are continuing widespread corruption, regulations for doing business which can be particularly strict (especially for foreign companies), the lack of sufficient quality and quantity of infrastructure, a higher level of bureaucracy adversely impacting the effectiveness and performance of good governance, the natural disasters which occur from time to time, and social instability. These remain some of the Indonesia-specific obstacles which foreign capital and foreign investment continue to struggle with. Nevertheless the implementation of increasingly liberal government legislation along with Indonesia's evolving digital landscape offers businesses a unique opportunity.

1.6.2 Exchange of Gifts

[46] In Indonesia, exchanges of gifts between business partners with established commercial relations are considered polite and involve a particular associated etiquette. However, some companies, especially those having an international background, have already introduced anti-corruption policies regarding the exchange of gifts or gratification. In addition, the donation of gifts to government officials, especially where related to their specific position, is not considered a normal feature and is therefore inadvisable.

[47] Indonesian people come with a wide diversity of local language, cultural, ethnic and religious backgrounds, and this creates its own problems, as the same language or gestures could mean different things to another ethnicity. However, Indonesians are in general very hospitable.

2 THE REGULATORY FRAMEWORK

2.1 Business Vehicles in Indonesia

2.1.1 The Forms of Business Vehicle

[48] In Indonesia, business entities are divided into those in the form of a legal entity (incorporated) and those not in the form of a legal entity (unincorporated) established in the territory of the Republic of Indonesia and carrying out businesses and/or activities in certain fields. A business entity in the form of a legal

entity means there is a separation between the assets of the founder(s) and that of the established entity. While a business entity not in the form of a legal entity means there is no separation between the assets of the founder(s) and that of the established entity.

[49] Examples of Business Entities in the Form of a Legal Entity include:

(i) Foundation (*Yayasan*)
(ii) Cooperative (*Koperasi*)
(iii) Limited Liability Company (*Perseroan Terbatas* (**PT**))
(iv) Public Listed Company – listed on the Indonesia Stock Exchange (*Perseroan Terbatas Terbuka or Perseroan Terbuka* (**PT Tbk**)
(v) State-Owned Company (*Badan Usaha Milik Negara* (BUMN) PT – ends with (Persero));
provincially or municipally owned corporations (*Badan Usaha Milik Daerah* (BUMD)).
(vi) Broadcasting Institution (*Lembaga Penyiaran*)

[50] Example of Business Entities Not in the Form of a Legal Entity include:

(i) Sole Proprietorship (*Usaha Dagang* (UD) *or perusahaan dagang* (PD)
(ii) Firms (*Firma*)
(iii) Civil Partnership (of professionals, e.g., doctors, accountants, lawyers) (*Persekutuan Perdata*)
(iv) Limited Partnership (*Persekutuan Komanditer* (CV)).

[51] The most common form of business vehicle used in Indonesia is the limited liability company (*Perseroan Terbatas* abbreviated '**PT**'). The PT is divided into two types, private and public companies. A private company is a legal entity that constitutes an alliance of capital established pursuant to a contract in order to carry on business activities with an authorized capital all of which is divided into shares, while the public company is a company whose shares are owned by at least 300 shareholders with a capital of at least IDR3 000 000 000 (approximately USD203 576), or several shareholders and paid-up capital stipulated by specific Government Regulation.

2.1.2 The Main Compliance Obligations on Registration and Reporting

[52] As regards the Limited Liability Company with Foreign Ownership (PT PMA), the main compliance requirements in terms of registration are:

(1) Creating and activating the Online Single Submission (OSS) account.
(2) Executing a deed of establishment in the Indonesian language before a public notary, and obtaining approval from the MoLHR for the establishment of the PT PMA.
(3) Obtaining a Business Identification Number (*Nomor Induk Berusaha*) (NIB), including Tax-ID, Health and Employment Insurance, Commercial License, etc.

(4) Issuing a statement by the PT PMA committing to fulfil the requirement to obtain a Location Permit, and the OSS System to issuing the Location Permit, Environment Permit or Building Permit. A Business Permit is automatically issued after the PT PMA states its commitment to finalize the prerequisite permits.
(5) Obtaining an operational/commercial license from the OSS System.

[53] The main compliance requirements for a PT PMA in terms of reporting are:

<table>
<tr><th>Business Investment Value</th><th>LKPM Submission Obligation</th><th>Remarks</th></tr>
<tr><td><IDR50m</td><td>Excluded from the LKPM submission obligation</td><td></td></tr>
<tr><td>IDR50m–IDR500m ('Investment Value I')</td><td>Required to submit LKPM semesterly</td><td></td></tr>
<tr><td>IDR500m–IDR10bn ('Investment Value II')</td><td>Required to submit LKPM quarterly</td><td rowspan="2">The LKPM should comprise:
(a) development/construction LKPM (if the business is still non-operational); and
(b) production/operation LKPM (if operations have already started).</td></tr>
<tr><td>>IDR10bn ('Investment Value III')</td><td>Required to submit LKPM quarterly</td></tr>
</table>

[54] Note that businesses operating within the following sectors: (a) oil and gas, (b) banking; (c) non-bank financial institutions; and (d) insurance are also excluded from the LKPM submission obligation.

(1) Companies engaged in the financial services sector must submit a monthly report and audited annual financial statement, as well as an annual business plan and an implementation of good corporate governance report, to the Indonesian OJK.
(2) Audited annual financial statements (*Laporan Keuangan Tahunan Perusahaan)* (**LKTP**) (including the balance sheet, profit and loss statement, cash flow report, statement of changes in equity and notes to the financial statement) must be submitted to the Ministry of Trade (MoT).
(3) Applicable taxes must be reported and paid to the tax office through online.
(4) A Mandatory Manpower Report must be submitted to the local manpower office, i.e., an annual Manpower Report *(Wajib Lapor Tenaga Kerja)*

(**WLTK**) and a Manpower Welfare Facility Report (*Wajib Lapor Fasilitas Kesejahteraan)* (**WLFK**).

(5) The Annual General Meeting of Shareholders (**AGMS**) of the company must be held within six months of the end of the financial year, as required by Indonesian law.

2.1.3 Minimum Share Capital Requirements of PT PMA

[55] To carry out business in Indonesia, foreign investment must be in the form of a PT, with the requirements to establish a PT set out in Law No. 40 of 2007 on Limited Liability Company as amended by Law No. 11 of 2020 on Job Creation ('**Law No. 40/2007 or the Company Law**'). Previously, according to the Company Law, the minimum authorized capital for a company was IDR50 000 000 (approximately USD3 400). However, Article 109 point 3 of the Job Creation Law amends the minimum authorized capital requirement for PT into 'to be determined based on the decision of the company founder'. Arrangements regarding this matter has been regulated in Government Regulation No. 8 of 2021 on Authorized Capital of Companies and Registration of Establishment, Amendment and Disbursement of Companies that Meet the Criteria for Micro and Small Businesses.

[56] However, since the shareholders of a PT PMA are foreign, the regulations dealing with large-scale and foreign investment also apply. According to Government Regulation No. 5 of 2021 on the Implementation of Risk-Based-Business Licensing ('**GR No. 5/2021**'), the PT PMA is required to satisfy a number of capital and investment-value prerequisites, as follows:

- the required total investment value must be more than IDR10bn (approximately USD678 500) excluding any immovable assets (land and buildings) per 5 digit the Indonesia Standard Industrial Classification ('KBLI') business sector per relevant project location;
- the amount of issued capital must be equivalent to the relevant paid-up capital and must be at least IDR2.5bn (approximately USD169 600);

(a) The provisions for the total investment as referred to above are exempted for several business activities as follows:
   (i) for large trading business activities, the required total investment value must be more than IDR10bn excluding land and buildings, is per 4 initial digits of KBLI;
   (ii) for food and drinks service business activities throughout open for foreign investment, the required total investment value must be more than IDR10bn excluding land and buildings, is per 2 initial digits of KBLI per 1 point location;
   (iii) for construction business activities throughout open for foreign investment, the required total investment value must be more than IDR10bn excluding land and buildings in one activity, is per 4 initial digits of KBLI; or

(iv) for industrial business activities which produce types of products with 5 different digits of KBLI in 1 production line, the required total investment value must be more than IDR10bn excluding land and buildings;

(b) share ownership percentages should be calculated based on the nominal value of the shares, unless otherwise provided by specific regulations covering, e.g., banking, insurance or freight forwarding businesses.

[57] The above prerequisites do not apply to PT PMAs which secured valid investment licenses before the issuance of GR No. 5/2021.

2.1.4 Management Structure of the PT

[58] The structure of the PT is a two-tier system comprising Board of Directors (BoD) charged with its day-to-day management, which is supervised by a Board of Commissioners (BoC). Based on Law No. 40/2007, the BoD may consist of one or more members, and where it consists of two or more members, the division of management tasks and authority between the members is determined in resolutions of the General Meeting of Shareholders (GMS), and one of the members is appointed as a president director. Sectoral regulations may require a specific number of directors and respective qualifications. Unlike the Anglo-Saxon system, there is no such position as a non-executive director. The duty to supervise the BoD is vested in the BoC, which is tasked with the supervision of the company policies, the general management of the company and its business, as well as advising the BoD.

[59] The BoD represent the company in and out of the courts as well as bearing responsibility for the management of the company. Except as stipulated otherwise in the company's articles of association (AoA), each director has the full power to bind and represent the company in all aspects (e.g., entering into contracts on the company's behalf and representing it in dispute settlements). However, the AoA or decisions of the BoD may limit the respective powers and duties of each director. The BoD has the authority to give a written power of attorney to one or more employees of the company or to some other persons for and on behalf of the company to perform specific legal actions if the BoD cannot represent the company.

2.2 Laws Affecting M&A

[60] The main laws and/or regulations involved in M&A activity in Indonesia include, among others:

- The Indonesian Civil Code (ICC).
- Law No. 11 of 2020 on Job Creation ('Law No. 11/2020 or the Job Creation Law').
- Law No. 40 of 2007 on Limited Liability Companies, as last amended by Law No. 11 of 2020 on Job Creation ('Law No. 40/2007 or the Company Law').
- Law No. 25 of 2007 on Capital Investment, as last amended by Law No. 11 of 2020 on Job Creation ('**Law No. 25/2007 or the Investment Law**').

- Law No. 13 of 2003 on Manpower, as last amended by Law No. 11 of 2020 on Job Creation ('**Law No. 13/2003**').
- Law No. 5 of 1999 on Prohibition of Monopolistic Practice and Unfair Business Competition as amended by Law No. 11 of 2020 on Job Creation ('**Law No. 5/1999 or the Antitrust Law**').
- Law No. 8 of 1995 on the Capital Market ('**Law No. 8/1995**').
- Law No. 5 of 1960 concerning Agrarian Matters ('**Law No. 5/1960**').
- Government Regulation No. 5 of 2021 on Implementation of Risk-Based Business Licensing ('**GR No. 5/2021**').
- Government Regulation No. 57 of 2010 on Merger or Consolidation of Business Entities and the Acquisition of Shares of Companies Which May Cause Monopolistic Practices and Unfair Business Competition ('**GR No. 57/2010**').
- Government Regulation No. 27 of 1998 on Merger, Consolidation, and Acquisition of a Limited Liability Company ('**GR No. 27/1998**').
- Presidential Regulation No. 13 of 2018 on Implementation of the Principle of Recognizing Beneficial Ownership of Corporations in the Framework of the Prevention and Eradication of Money Laundering and Criminal Acts of Terrorism Financing ('**PR No. 13/2018**').
- Presidential Regulation No. 10 of 2021 on Investment Business Activities ('**PR No. 10/2021**').
- Investment Coordinating Board (BKPM) Regulation No. 6 of 2018 on Guidelines and Procedures of Licensing and Investment Facilities as amended by BKPM Regulation No. 5 of 2019 ('**BKPM Regulation No. 6/2018**').
- The Indonesian Business Competition Supervisory Commission (KPPU) Regulation No. 3 of 2019 on Assessment of Merger or Consolidation of Business Entities or Acquisition of Company Shares which may Result in Monopolistic Practices and Unfair Business Competition ('**KPPU Regulation No. 3/2019**').
- Various tax laws.

[61] The general laws and/or regulations involved in M&A activity set by the Company Law apply to all companies. However, there are also different laws/regulations applicable to specific types of company or different types of transaction, namely:

- Financial Service Authority (OJK) Regulation No. 12/POJK.03/2020 on the Consolidation of Commercial Banks ('**OJK Regulation No. 12/2020**').
- OJK Regulation No. 41/POJK.03/2019 on Merger, Consolidation, Acquisition, Integration, And Conversion of Commercial Banks ('**OJK Regulation No. 41/2019**').
- OJK Regulation No. 21/POJK.03/2019 on Mergers, Consolidations, Acquisition of Rural Banks and Sharia Rural Banks ('**OJK Regulation No. 21/2019**').
- OJK Regulation No. 9/POJK.04/2018 on the Acquisition of Public Companies ('**OJK Regulation No. 9/2018**').

- OJK Regulation No. 74/POJK.04/2016 as last amended by POJK No. 58/POJK.04/2017 on Mergers or Consolidations of Public Company ('**OJK Regulation No. 74/2016**').
- OJK Regulation No. 54/POJK.04/2015 on Voluntary Tender Offers ('**OJK Regulation No. 54/2015**').
- Any other regulations depending on the nature of the business of the target or the purchaser, such as banking, forestry and mining.

[62] The main differences between private deals and public deals are as follows. Private deals are regulated less strictly than public deals in terms of (*inter alia*) disclosure issues. A public company will be monitored by the OJK and will be subject to specific OJK Regulation. A further important difference is that in a private deal there is a seller to indemnify the buyer and/or to stand behind its obligations following the transaction's close. However, in a public deal, there will typically be no identifiable party to stand behind the obligations of the target after closing.

[63] Neither Law No. 40/2007 nor any other laws and regulations on M&A in Indonesia specifically regulate situations where the target company's BoD or Shareholders resist the takeover. Nor do they recognize the term 'Friendly/Agreed or Hostile Transactions'. The concept of the hostile transaction is not common in Indonesia.

[64] Under the laws and regulations in Indonesia, the main ways in which companies and businesses can combine and divide are in the forms of merger, tender offer, and acquisition of shares of private companies and businesses.

[65] Corporate governance frameworks typically comprise elements of the legislation, regulations, voluntary commitments, self-regulatory arrangements, and business practices. Some companies in Indonesia have voluntary corporate governance codes or guidelines in addition to their AoA. Most codes/guidelines are brief and simple statements of principle that generally reflect the desire of the BoC and the BoD to conduct company operations in an honest, fair, legal and socially responsible manner.

2.3 Relevant Regulatory Authorities

[66] The following are the main governmental/regulatory authorities and their respective responsibilities.

2.3.1 Ministry of Law and Human Rights (MoLHR)

[67] In relation to merger and acquisition transactions, MoLHR is responsible for providing approval on ratification of the company as a legal entity; approval on the amendment of AoA of companies and the management of the company registry. In addition, the MoLHR must be notified of changes in the shareholding structure of companies.

2.3.2 Indonesia Coordinating Investment Board (BKPM)

[68] BKPM as the OSS Agency is responsible for providing regulations on investment in Indonesia and issues licences relating to investment such as the NIB and the Business License, as well as Commercial or Operational Licenses for and on behalf of Ministries, Heads of Agencies, Governors, Regents and Mayors; conducting an integrated one-stop service for the provision of licences (or denial of licences) to the investor.

2.3.3 Financial Services Authority (OJK)

[69] OJK is responsible for providing regulations on financial services in Indonesia for financial as well as non-financial institutions operating in the capital market sector and providing approval for transactions in the financial service sector including merger and acquisition transactions.

2.3.4 The Commission for the Supervision of Business Competition (KPPU)

[70] The KPPU is charged with the supervision of business competition pursuant to Law No. 5/1999 on the Prohibition of Monopoly Practices and Unfair Business Competition. It is an independent commission, directly responsible to the President. Specifically, its tasks include:

(a) Evaluating agreements that may result in monopoly practice or unfair business competition.
(b) Evaluating business practice or the conduct of business actors that may result in monopoly or unfair business competition practices.
(c) Evaluating whether or not a dominant position is being abused that may result in a monopoly or unfair business practices.
(d) Taking actions to address monopoly or unfair business practices, including receiving complaints, investigating, summoning business players, obtaining documents, and imposing administrative sanctions.
(e) Issuing recommendations and opinions on government policy in relation to government policies on monopoly and unfair business practices.
(f) Issuing draft guidance and/or publications in relation to Law No. 5/1999.
(g) Reporting the result of the Commission's work to the President and the People's Legislative Council (DPR).

2.3.5 Industry-Specific Regulators

[71] Depending on the business sector and the relevant corporate action, notification, recommendation, or even approval from industry regulators may be necessary. As an example, the purchase of the shares of a bank that results in more than

40% of the shares being owned by one financial institution requires the approval of OJK.

2.3.6 Local Government (Provincial and/or Regency/City)

[72] Within the framework of investment in Indonesia, local government may have a role to play in providing approvals if the relevant powers have been delegated to it in accordance with its authority. Based on the implementation of regional autonomy, the relevant local government may issue laws and regulations on matters including those relating to merger and acquisition transactions.

[73] The investor can engage personally to follow up with the relevant regulatory authorities to attempt to expedite the process. However, the investor may also delegate this process to other parties to handle provided there is a power of attorney. There is no differentiation in the timetable to obtain government approval, whether this is conducted by the investor itself and/or through its advisers, although advisors who specialize in certain approvals will be more familiar with the specific requirements and actual practices.

2.4 Controls/Restrictions on Foreign Investment

2.4.1 Restriction on Foreign Investment

[74] Indonesia is open for foreign investment. The principle of Law No. 25/2007 is that all business sectors are open to investment, both by foreign and by domestic investors, unless they are closed or with certain requirements by law, or they involve activities that can only be carried out by the central government. There are several sectors that are closed or otherwise with certain requirements to foreign investment. Pursuant to Article 12 of Law No. 25/2007 which has been amended by Law 11/2020, the business sectors that are closed for foreign investors are:

(a) the cultivation and industry of category I narcotics;
(b) all forms of gambling and/or casino activities;
(c) the capture of fish species listed under Appendix I of the Convention on International Trade in Endangered Species of Wild Fauna and Flora (CITES);
(d) the utilization or taking of corals and the utilization or taking of reefs from nature;
(e) the chemical weapon manufacturing industry; and
(f) the chemical industry and the ozone-depleting substance industry.

[75] Note that all foreign direct investment activities must be carried out through a PT unless investment through an alternative vehicle is permitted by law. We understand that in the following sectors, business activities conducted through a vehicle other than a PT are possible:

(a) banking;
(b) construction services; and
(c) oil and gas exploration and exploitation.

[76] Foreign interests of companies are denominated in terms of the percentage of the company's shares. The priority business fields, allocated business fields or partnership with cooperatives and micro, small, and medium enterprises, and business fields that are open with certain requirements (e.g., maximum foreign shareholding and other conditions) on foreign investment in Indonesia, business fields that are not included in the three types of business fields above – in which all investors are allowed to invest in are regulated under the Positive Investment List, which is set out under Annexes I,II, and III of PR No. 10/2021. Additionally, the following material restrictions are applicable pursuant to other laws and regulations:

(a) Defence: ownership of capital based on the approval of the minister of defence.
(b) Insurance: the maximum foreign ownership is 80%, although a larger percentage can be held depending on the capital structure.
(c) Banking: the maximum foreign ownership is 99% but subject to certain restrictions on the number of shares that any shareholder may hold and a special licence from OJK.
(d) Finance companies: the maximum foreign ownership is 80%–85%.
(e) Nuclear and other energy power plants: the maximum foreign ownership is 95%.
(f) Transportation: the maximum foreign ownership is 49%.
(g) Communication markets: for newspapers (domestic capital must be 100% for the establishment and maximum foreign capital 49% through capital market for business expansion and development), for private broadcasting agency for TV and radio (only for business expansion and development) the maximum foreign capital ownership is 20%, and for other media the domestic capital must be 100% for the establishment and maximum foreign capital 20% through capital market for business expansion and development.

2.4.2 Foreign Ownership Restrictions

[77] A foreign investor may (by the acquisition of an existing company or the establishment of a new one) own 100% of shares in an Indonesian company unless it is restricted by law.

[78] As discussed above, the principle of Indonesia's investment policy is that all business sectors are open to investment unless the relevant sector is closed or restricted (partially open) by the applicable law. With the exception of a few sectors, all foreign investment activities must be conducted through a PT, formed in accordance with the provisions of Law No. 40/2007. Foreign investors' interests are denominated in terms of the percentage of paid-up capital in such PT(s) owned by that foreign investor. In turn, the maximum percentage of foreign shareholding in the restricted sectors must conform to the requirements of the Positive Investment List (currently PR No. 10/2021).

[79] A domestic capital investment company is distinguished from a foreign investment company by whether or not a foreign person or entity owns any shares of the PT. If the answer is yes, the PT will be deemed to be a Foreign Investment Company (PT PMA). This classification does not factor in the percentage of the shares owned, with the consequence that any share ownership by a foreign person or an entity in a PT, irrespective of how little, results in the PT being classified as a PT PMA. Furthermore, the positive investment list does not discriminate between the acquisition of shares in an existing company and the creation of a new company. As such, any locally established SPV corporation whose shares are owned by a foreigner will be classified as a PT PMA and thus subject to the positive investment list, irrespective of the foreign-owned percentage.

[80] Previously, as a matter of procedure to perfect investors' rights, every corporate action involving a change in the shareholding composition had to be reported to and approved by both the MoLHR and the BKPM. However, under Government Regulation No. 24 of 2018 on Electronically Integrated Business Licensing Services which was revoked by GR No. 5/2021, with the new OSS system, business actors are not required to obtain any prior approval from the OSS agency, i.e., from BKPM. This creates a post-audit nature of the system, whereby the audit by BKPM or by relevant ministries for compliance with regard to relevant corporate actions involving a company (e.g., establishment, change of shareholders of a company, change of capital structure of a company and/or conversion of a PMDN company into a PMA company), the fulfilment of commitments and other forms of monitoring and control will be conducted after such activity has been undertaken by the company.

[81] For these reasons, the acquisition by way of purchase of the shares of the target company through a locally formed SPV raises a number of significant legal issues. First, the SPV will be classified as a PT PMA, and it will therefore itself be subject to the positive investment list. Second, even if the SPV serves merely as a holding company to own the shares of the target company, the action will be typically carried out through a sale and purchase of shares. Such corporate actions must be reported to, and in some cases require approval from, various regulators. Such actions typically require disclosure of the shareholding structure.

[82] In certain sectors, particularly those likely to be exposed to significant regulatory overhead and/or a history of corrupt practices, the valuation expectations of vendors can be entirely unrealistic. This is due to a view that it is impossible for an outsider to secure the assets/licenses that they hold, and often the fact that the assets/licenses were secured by the owners at minimal cost, resulting in little downside to holding out for a future potential transaction (this is particularly true of mineral concessions). Additionally, and generally, silent partners are a prevalent feature in certain sectors, resulting in an agreement for a transaction having to be secured not only from the actual shareholders of the target but also from 'stakeholders' who have influence over the shareholders.

[83] According to Law No. 25/2007, domestic investors and foreign investors investing in a limited liability company are prohibited from entering into an agreement and/or making a statement asserting that the ownership of shares in that company is for and on behalf of another person (nominee agreement). In the event that investors enter into such an agreement and/or make such a statement, such agreement and/or statement shall be declared as null and void.

2.4.3 Formal Approvals

[84] The company (or target company) will be subject to and must comply with at least three regimes of formal approvals. The categories of permit regimes are:

(1) Approvals and corporate documents related to the company.
(2) Approvals to conduct business operations.
(3) Approvals related to foreign investment.

[85] In relation to the costs involved in the formal approval process, the key costs are the notary fee, the legal and/or financial advisor service fee (if any), and the non-tax revenue fee for some business licences (if any). In terms of the length of time the process will take, this may depend on the negotiation and due diligence process. From a regulatory perspective it is likely to be at least three months for a private M&A transaction.

Approvals and Corporate Documents Related to the Company

[86] The procedure for incorporation is a two-stage process. First, the company incorporators (founding shareholders) enter into an agreement to incorporate, formalized by a notarial deed before a public notary. Second, the incorporators apply for recognition from the Government to ratify the company incorporation.

Document Name	*Issuing Authority*	*Time to Issue*[2]	*Official Cost (IDR)*
The company's deed of establishment and Article of Association	*Notary Public*	*1–2 days*	*Vary*

[2] Time to issue means the length of time after the required documents are submitted and deemed to be complete and correct. The issuance time does not take into account the verification process.

Document Name	*Issuing Authority*	*Time to Issue*[2]	*Official Cost (IDR)*
Legalization of the establishment of the company. (SK *Pengesahan*)	Minister of Law and Human Rights (handled by the notary)	Within a maximum period of 14 days	The non-tax revenue fee is IDR100 000 to check the company's name and IDR500 000 up to IDR1 000 000 for legalization of the establishment of the company as a legal entity + IDR580 000 for the Official Gazette of the Republic of Indonesia)
Taxpayer Identification Number (NPWP)	Director General of Tax (the OSS system is integrated with the system at the DGT)	1 Day	–
Social Security on Health and Employment	The Social Security Agency/BPJS (the OSS system is integrated with the system at the BPJS)	7 days	–

[87] Under Law No. 40/2007, a company only attains its status as a legal entity once the MoLHR has recognized its existence, thus the separate company's liability and the capacity to take legal actions and to own assets and bear liabilities on its own behalf. Recognition of existence is formalized when the minister issues the legalization on the establishment of the company (*SK Pengesahan Pendirian Badan Hukum Perseroan Terbatas*). To obtain the legalization on the establishment of the company, the incorporator or its agent must first reserve a name at the MoLHR to ensure that it has not been used by another Indonesian company, to avoid rejection by the MoLHR of the company's deed of establishment and AoA. Amendments to the company's AoA must be reported to or, in certain cases, require approval from the MoLHR. The relevant amendments are listed below:

No.	*Change to AoA*	*Reporting*	*Approval*
1	Name and Domicile of the company	✓	✓
2	Purpose and Business sector of the Company	✓	✓
3	Duration of Establishment	✓	✓
4	Amount of Authorized Capital	✓	✓
5	Reduction of the Amount of Subscribed Capital	✓	✓
6	Reduction of the Paid-Up Capital	✓	✓
7	Change of Status from a Public to a Private Company and Vice Versa	✓	✓
8	Change to Current Shareholders Percentage That Causes a Change in Control of the Company (Without Changes to the Amount of Authorized, Subscribed or Paid-Up Capital)	✓	✓
9	Changes to AoA as part of a Merger or Acquisition	✓	✓
10	Changes of Shareholder due to a Transfer of Shares and/or a Change in the Number of Shares Owned (That Does not Cause a Change of Control of the Company)	✓	
11	Other changes	✓	

[88] Law No. 40/2007 does not prescribe any penalty for failure to report. However, it is to be noted that the ownership of shares, and the rights attached thereto, are only perfected and become enforceable against third parties upon the letter of recognition or ratification by the MoLHR.

Approvals to Conduct Business Operations

[89] Every business actor including a foreign-owned company/PT PMA, which engages in trade business activities, must fulfil the business licensing requirements of the central government of Indonesia through the OSS. The Job Creation Law introduces a new concept of business license. The concept of a business license (license approach) is changed from the application of standard-based to a risk-based approach (RBA). The application of Risk-Based Business Licensing is to improve the investment ecosystem and business activities, besides the simplification of business licensing requirements.

[90] Risk-Based Business Licensing is carried out based on a determination of the relevant risk level and business scale rating of business activities, which are obtained on the basis of assessments of hazard level and hazard potential by looking into the following aspects – health; safety; environment; and/or utilization and management of resources. According to GR No. 5/2021, the implementation of risk-based business licensing covering following sectors:

(1) marine and fisheries;
(2) agriculture;
(3) environment and forestry;
(4) energy and mineral resources;
(5) nuclear power;
(6) industry;
(7) trading;
(8) public work and public housing;
(9) transportation;
(10) health, medicine and food;
(11) education and culture;
(12) tourism;
(13) religious matter;
(14) post, telecommunication, broadcasting and electronic systems and transactions;
(15) defense and security; and
(16) employment.

	Risk-Based Business Licensing	
Low-Risk Activities	Business registration only in the form of Business Identification Number (*Nomor Induk Berusaha*/ 'NIB').	
Medium–Low-Risk Activities	Business registration and a statement letter of fulfilment of business standards.	
Medium–High-Risk Activities	Business registration and business standards certificate from the central or regional Government.	Standard assessment (compliance) is carried out by a certified profession.

High-Risk Activities	Business registration, license in the form of an approval issued by the central or regional Government, and standard certifications.	High-risk business activities are business activities that have an impact on health, safety, and the environment as well as natural resource management activities. The government carries out strict supervision and inspection of high-risk business activities.

Document Name	*Issuing Authority*	*Time to Issue*[3]	*Official Cost (IDR, 000)*
Business Identification Number (*Nomor Induk Berusaha*/'NIB'). The other functions of NIB, as: 1. a company registration; 2. an import identification numbers; 3. a custom access; and 4. initial submission of Mandatory Manpower Report.	The OSS System managed by the BKPM.	Automatically issued after business owner has fulfilled the requirements/commitments.	Some are free, and some are with fee requirement.
Business License		Business license is issued after the commitment of location permit, environment permit/SPPL, building permit, SLF and any other business license prerequisites have been fulfilled and the payment (if required) has been completed. Vary between 1 and 15 days	
Commercial/Operational License.		Operational/commercial licenses are issued automatically after the commitment statement is filed but only take effect after the commitment has been fulfilled, including the relevánt payment (if required). Vary between 1 and 15 days	

[3] Time to issue means the length of time after the required documents are submitted and deemed to be complete and correct. The issuance time does not take into account the verification process.

[91] Furthermore, BKPM Regulation No.1/2020 has categorized types of issuance of Business Licenses and Commercial/Operational Licenses into several classifications as follows:

(a) without commitment fulfilment, where the OSS institution will issue a business license and commercial/operational license that will be effective immediately;
(b) subject to technical requirements;
(c) subject to fee requirements;
(d) subject to technical and fee requirements.

[92] For types (b), (c), and (d) the OSS institution will issue an effective business license and commercial/operational license once the specific requirements have been completed by the applicant.

Approvals Related to Foreign Investment

Document Name	*Issuing Authority*	*Time to Issue (days)*	*Cost (IDR) (Official Cost)*
– Foreign representative office registration (*Pendaftaran KPPA*), – foreign trade representative office license (*Izin KP3A*), – foreign construction service company license (*Izin BUJKA*), – Franchisee registration certificate of a franchisor coming from abroad; – futures trader registration; and – registration of Administrative Branch Offices.	OSS Institution	5 days	–

Document Name	*Issuing Authority*	*Time to Issue (days)*	*Cost (IDR) (Official Cost)*
Foreign Worker Recruitment Plan (*Rencana Penggunaan Tenaga Kerja Asing* – 'RPTKA')	Ministry of Manpower (https://tka-online.kemnaker.go.id/)	3 days	–
- Limited Stay Visa (VITAS) for shareholders; - Temporary Stay Permit (ITAS); - Permanent Stay Permit (ITAP).	Directorate General of Immigration (http://izintinggal.imigrasi.go.id/IT-online)	7–14 days	For VITAS: IDR300 000 For ITAS: IDR450 000–IDR1 600 000 For ITAP: IDR3 500 000–IDR10 200 000

2.4.4 Restriction on Foreign Directors or Managers

[93] A foreigner may fill positions within BoD and BoC, provided that such positions do not relate to matters pertaining to human resources and do not conflict with any prevailing laws and regulations. Pursuant to the Minister of Manpower Decree No. 349 of 2019 on Certain Positions Restricted for Expatriates, 18 positions are restricted for expatriates to hold, among others the position of Personnel Director. This regulation removes the Chief Executive Officer position from the list of restricted positions governed by the previous regulations.

[94] On the other hand, the Minister of Manpower Decree No. 228 of 2019 on Certain Positions Available to Expatriates sets out lists of 2 196 positions available for expatriates. The positions are divided into 18 business sectors, namely: (1) Construction; (2) Real Estate; (3) Education; (4) Processing Industry; (5) Water Management, Waste-Water Management, Waste Management and Recycling, and Remediation Activities; (6) Transportation and Warehousing; (7) Arts, Entertainment, and Recreation; (8) Provision of Accommodation and Provision of Food and Beverages; (9) Agriculture, Forestry and Fisheries; (10) Renting and Leasing without Option Rights, Employment, Travel Agents and Other Supporting Businesses; (11) Financial and Insurance Activities; (12) Human Health Activities and Social Activities; 13) Information and Telecommunications; (14) Mining and Extraction; (15) Procurement of Electricity, Gas, Hot Water/Vapor and Cold Air; (16) Wholesale and Retail, Reparation and Maintenance of Cars and Motorcycle; (17) Activities Involving Other Services; and (18) Activities in the Professional, Scientific and Technical Sectors.

[95] For some business fields, the industries are limited to local companies (small-, micro, and medium-scale enterprises) and partnership between local and foreign companies, such as forest business (bamboo, etc.), fishery product processing business.

2.4.5 Restrictions on a Foreigner or Foreign-Owned Company Owning Land, Mining/Mineral Rights

[96] In conducting business in Indonesia, foreign investors (meaning foreigners residing in Indonesia, or corporate bodies established under Indonesian Law and based in Indonesia, and foreign companies which have a representative office in Indonesia) cannot have a Right to Own Land (Hak Milik). Instead, they are permitted to own subsidiary land rights. Indonesia's land law regime divides rights over land into a hierarchy of rights. A foreigner is permitted to own two specific land rights, which are Leasehold (Article 45 Law No. 5/1960) and the Right to Use (Article 41 Law No. 5/1960). Furthermore, Foreign Investment Companies (PT PMAs) may utilize three different types of land right for their business activities, namely a Right to Cultivate, a Right to Build, or a Right to Use based on Article 22 Law No. 25/2007 on Investments, for a specified period by means of the following rights:

- The Right to Cultivate (*Hak Guna Usaha* or HGU), for agricultural, fishery or animal husbandry purposes, is granted for a maximum period of thirty-five years and can be extended for a maximum period of twenty-five years. A PT PMA (a foreign direct investment company) that needs a longer period may be granted a renewal of the Right to Cultivate on the same land for a maximum period of thirty-five years.
- The Right to Build (*Hak Guna Bangunan* or HGB) is a right to build and to own buildings on land which is not one's own property for no longer than thirty years, and this can be extended by a period no longer than twenty years.
- The Right to Use (*Hak Pakai*) is a right to use and/or to collect the produce of land directly controlled by the state, or of land owned by other persons, subject to the specific rights and obligations stipulated in the decision of the authorized official granting such right, or in the agreement to work the land, in so far as it does not conflict with the spirit and letter of the law. It is granted for a maximum period of twenty-five years, and can be extended for twenty years, or granted for an unspecified period provided the land is used for certain specific purposes.

[97] Foreign investors are permitted to own mining/mineral rights. For general mining, 100% foreign ownership is permitted. However, there is an obligation to divest 51% gradually over a five-year period after five years of commercial production has taken place. The timeline requires companies to divest at least 20% of their shares after six years, 30% after seven years, 37% after eight years, 44% after nine years and 51% after ten years.

2.5 Incentives for Foreign Investment

2.5.1 Grants or Investment Incentives Available to Foreign Investors

[98] To begin with, incentives for the foreign investor are stipulated under Law No. 25 of 2007 concerning Investment as amended by Law No. 11 of 2020 concerning Job Creation ('**Law No. 25/2007**') by which the government grants incentives to investors who expand their businesses and make new investments. The incentives are granted to a foreign investor who fulfils at least one of the requirements below:

(a) absorbs many workers;
(b) falls within a high priority sector;
(c) is engaged in infrastructure construction;
(d) carries out technology transfer;
(e) is engaged in a pioneer industry;
(f) is located in a remote or less-developed area, a border area, or another area deemed needy;
(g) preserves environmental sustainability;
(h) conducts research, development, and innovation activities;
(i) is in partnership with micro, small, and medium enterprises or cooperatives;
(j) is engaged in an industry that uses domestically produced capital goods or machines or equipment; and/or
(k) falls within the business of tourism development.

2.5.2 Special Tax Exemptions

[99] The incentives can be granted in the form of income tax relief by a reduction of net income to a specified extent of the total investments made within a specified period; exemptions or reliefs on import duty for the production of capital goods, machines, or equipment not yet produced at home; exemptions or reliefs on import duty for the production of raw materials or components for a specified period and subject to specified requirements; exemptions or deferment of Value Added Tax (VAT) for a specified period on the import of capital goods, machines or equipment not yet produced at home; accelerated depreciation or amortization; and relief from land and buildings tax, particularly for specified business sectors in specified regions or areas or zones. Nevertheless, each incentive, as referred to above, is granted subject to particular conditions depending on the particular circumstances of the relevant business. Additionally, the government provides qualifying investment companies with a simplified service and/or with permissions to obtain land titles, immigration service facilities; and import permission facilities.

[100] Pursuant to Government Regulation No. 78 of 2019 on Income Tax Facilities for Investments within Certain Business Sectors and/or within Certain Regions ('**Government Regulation No. 78/2019**') and further provision in the Minister of

Finance Regulation No. 11/PMK.010/2020 concerning the Implementation of Government Regulation No. 78/2019 as amended by the Minister of Finance Regulation No. 96/PMK.010/2020 ('**Minister of Finance Regulation No. 11/2020**') the incentives can be granted in the form of income tax through a reduction of net income by 30% of the value of total investments in the form of tangible fixed assets including land used for core business activities. The reduction is charged within a period of six years by 5% each year; accelerated deprecation over tangible fixed assets and accelerated amortization over intangible assets which are obtained in the context of investment; the imposition of income tax of 10% on dividends paid to foreign tax residents other than those having a permanent establishment in Indonesia, or a lower rate according to any applicable Double-Tax Avoidance Agreement; compensation for losses of more than five years but not more than ten years. Nevertheless, each incentive, as referred to above, is granted subject to particular conditions depending on the individual circumstances of each business. Additionally, the government provides investment companies with a simplified service and/or with permissions to obtain land titles, immigration service facilities; and import permission facilities.

[101] As regards special tax exemptions, the foreign investor is able to benefit from tax advantages under the Head of Indonesia Investment Coordinating Board Regulation No. 5 of 2019 on the Amendment of The Head of Indonesia Investment Coordinating Board Regulation No. 6 of 2018 on Guidelines and Procedures for Licenses and Facilities in Investment ('BKPM Regulation No. 5/2019'). These tax advantages include, *inter alia*:

(a) the grant of import facilitation for machinery, capital goods and materials for investment in the industrial sector and in the services sector;
(b) the grant of import facilitation for machinery and capital goods for the electricity sector;
(c) the grant of import facilitation for machinery and capital goods for contracts of work and for coal mining concession agreements;
(d) proposals for release or reduction of corporate income tax (tax holiday); and
(e) proposals for corporate income tax allowances for investment in specific businesses and/or in particular areas.

[102] Further, the Head of Indonesia Investment Coordinating Board of Investment Regulation No. 6 of 2019 on the Amendment of the Head of Indonesia Investment Coordinating Board of Investment Regulation No. 1 of 2019 sets out details of the business sectors and types of pioneer industry that can be given the facility of tax reduction on corporate income tax and establishes guidelines and procedures for the grant of tax reduction facilities on corporate income tax ('**BKPM Regulation No. 6/2019**'). Therefore, BKPM Regulation No. 6/2019 needs to be taken into consideration to determine the tax facilities available for the pioneer industry.

[103] In addition, in Law No. 7 of 1983 on Income Tax, as last amended by the Job Creation Law, it is stated that dividends or other income are exempted from tax subject to certain conditions:

(i) domestic dividends (whereas the previous law had stipulated these to be subject to 10% income tax);
(ii) dividends originating from overseas and after-tax income from an overseas permanent establishment received or obtained by a domestic corporate taxpayer or a domestic individual taxpayer (whereas the previous law had stipulated these to be subject to 5%–30% income tax);

as long as they are invested or used to support other business activities in the territory of the Republic of Indonesia within a certain period.

2.5.3 Special Economic Zones, Free Zones or Other Regions Offering Special Investment Incentives

[104] In Indonesia there are several zones offering special investment incentives including, among others, free trade zones, special economic zones, and bonded storage locations.

[105] First, Free Trade and Free Ports Zones in Indonesia are located in Batam, Bintan, and Karimun. Goods entering into and goods delivered between free trade areas are exempted from import duty and excise duty. In addition, no import taxes (including VAT, local service tax or income tax) are collected on these goods. Goods originating from a free trade area entering the Indonesian customs area are liable to import duties and taxes. Free ports are areas separate from the customs area and which as a result are free from the imposition of customs duties, VAT, and tax on luxury goods and customs.

[106] Second, in order to accelerate economic development and job growth, the government enacted Law No. 39 of 2009 on Special Economic Zones as last amended by the Job Creation Law ('Law No. 39/2009'). This defines zones within certain boundaries in the territories of the Unitary State of the Republic of Indonesia, which are designated to carry out economic activities and to which are granted certain facilities and incentives. Under Law No. 39/2009, business enterprises or business actors who conduct business within such a zone can be granted facilities and reliefs in terms of taxable income according to the type of business in question. Facilities granted in relation to special economic zones also include custom and excise facilities; exemptions or reliefs from regional taxes and regional levies; reliefs and acceleration in respect of land rights, business permits, immigration, investment, employment as well as other facilities and reliefs.

[107] Moreover, in accordance with Government Regulation No. 40 of 2021 on Implementation of Special Economic Zones ('Government Regulation No. 40/2021') business enterprises or business actors carrying on business within special economic zones can be granted facilities and reliefs in the form of tax, customs and excise; goods traffic; employment; immigration; land and spatial layout; business permits; and/or other facilities and reliefs.

[108] However, the facilities and reliefs referred to above are available only for business enterprises or business actors carrying on certain specified business activities, as set out in further detail below:

Government Regulation No. 40/2021	*Law No. 39/2009 as Amended by the Job Creation Law*
Production and processing; logistics and distribution; research, digital economy, and technology development; tourism; education; health; sport; financial services; creative industry; energy development; development and management of SEZ; and/or other economic activities.	Production and processing; logistics and distribution; technology development; tourism; education; health; energy; and/or other economic activities.

[109] Third, Bonded Storage Places. A Bonded Storage Place is a building, site or area meeting certain requirements which is used to store goods for certain specified purposes and which obtains import duty postponement. It is expected that the introduction of the Bonded Logistics Centre will encourage investment in the manufacturing sector in Indonesia because these centres will facilitate the flow of basic raw materials.

2.5.4 Government Guarantees Against Expropriation or Nationalization

[110] Under the Investment Law, the government of the Republic of Indonesia will not take any measures of nationalization or expropriation against proprietary rights of investors, unless provided by law. Furthermore, in the event that nationalization or expropriation needs to be conducted, the government of the Republic of Indonesia will provide fair compensation as determined by the market price. The market price is to be determined based on international practices and is established by independent appraisers appointed by the Government and the investor(s). It is of note that the law does not explicitly provide for the method of calculation, in particular whether or not the compensation price is based on the current market price of the expropriated asset or whether it takes into account expected future prices.

[111] If there is no consent between the parties concerning compensation or indemnity, settlement may be conducted through an arbitration process. Furthermore, according to bilateral investment treaties entered into by the Republic of Indonesia and other states, expropriation or nationalization may only take place under the following conditions:

(a) The measures must be taken for a lawful purpose or public purpose and under due process of law.
(b) The measures must be non-discriminatory.
(c) The measures must be accompanied by provision for the payment of prompt, adequate and effective compensation and must equate to the fair market

value without delay and prior to the measure of dispossession becoming public knowledge. Such market value must be determined in accordance with internationally acknowledged practices or methods. In the event that such fair market value cannot be determined, it must be such reasonable amount as may be mutually agreed between the parties, and it must be transferred in freely convertible/freely usable currency.

2.5.5 Payment of Dividends Abroad and Repatriation of Profits

[112] The payment of dividends abroad, the repatriation of profits and/or the proceeds of liquidation or sale, the payment of interest on foreign loans, the payment of fees and charges to foreign companies for IP or technology transfer are covered by Law No. 25/2007. In principle companies and businesses are entitled to transfer their own assets to their investors according to prevailing law.

[113] Under Law No. 25/2007 as amended by Law No. 11/2020, investors are granted rights to transfer and repatriate in foreign currencies capital, profits, bank interest, dividends, and other income; funds that are needed to purchase raw materials and components, intermediate goods or finished goods, goods to replace capital goods in order to protect the viability of the investments; additional funds needed for investment financing; funds for the repayment of loans; royalties and fees payable; income of foreign nationals working for an investment company; proceeds of the sale or liquidation of an investment; compensation for damages; compensation for acquisitions; payments made in connection with technical assistance, fees payable for technical and management services, payments made under a project contract, payments related to intellectual property rights (IPRs); and proceeds of the sale of assets as mentioned above.

[114] These actions need to be conducted according to the prevailing law and regulations. In cases where investors have not yet fulfilled their legal responsibilities, an investigator or Minister of Finance may request banks or other institutions to defer the right to transfer and/or to repatriate, and the court will have jurisdiction to order deferment of the rights of transfer and/or of repatriation following a claim. The deferment continues until the investor has discharged all its responsibilities.

[115] As regards the prevailing law and regulation on the use of foreign currency, BI has issued BI Regulation No. 17/3/PBI/2015 concerning the Obligation to Use Rupiah in the Territory of the Republic of Indonesia ('BI Regulation No. 17/2015') which obliges all payments and transactions conducted in the territory of Indonesia to use rupiah currency. Therefore, all such payments must be conducted using rupiah currency. Additionally, it should be noted that the transfer of investors' assets is without prejudice to the rights of the government to:

(a) require reporting of the funds transfers;
(b) draw tax, royalties and/or other government revenues from investments;
(c) protect the rights of creditors under applicable law;

(d) implement the law in order to prevent losses to the state.

[116] Finally, one should note that the Minister of Finance or state investigator (the police, the Attorney General's Office, and/or other civil service departments charged with the investigation) may request a bank to withhold the transfer pending fulfilment of the investor's obligations to the state. Equally, the court may impose a hold on any transfer and order the bank to withhold the transfer based on legal proceedings brought against the investor. Banks and other institutions in receipt of any such court order must comply.

2.5.6 Financing Options for Acquisitions in Indonesia

[117] The financing of an acquisition in Indonesia may be conducted through a loan and/or a syndicated loan, depending on the size of the transaction. Reasons for using a syndicated loan are to spread out the risk of the transaction and to avoid the Legal Lending Limit, because the participation in syndicated loans by one or more creditors/lending institutions allows for a larger loan amount and a longer loan period.

[118] A domestic bank may undertake to lend for large-scale investment; however, domestic commercial banks have a limitation on their ability to provide lending facilities as stated in BI Regulation No. 8/13/PBI/2006 regarding the amendment of BI Regulation No. 7/3/PBI/2005 concerning the Legal Lending Limit for Commercial Banks ('BI Regulation No. 8/2006'). The limitation is categorized into several conditions below:

(a) The prescribed maximum limit of the entire portfolio of Provision of Funds to Related Parties must be no more than 10% of the Bank's Capital.
(b) The prescribed maximum limit of Provision of Funds to one Borrower (not being a Related Party) must be no more than 20% of the Bank's Capital.
(c) The prescribed maximum limit of Provision of Funds to one Borrower group (not being a Related Party) must be no more than 25% of the Bank's Capital.

[119] However, pursuant to BI Regulation No. 18/19/PBI/2016 concerning Foreign Exchange Transactions Against Rupiah Between Banks and Foreign Parties, Banks are prohibited from carrying out transactions with Foreign Parties, including among others:

(a) the extension of credit or financing in rupiah and/or in foreign currency;
(b) deposits in Rupiah;
(c) purchase of Securities in rupiah issued by a foreign party;
(d) inter-office invoicing in rupiah;
(e) inter-office invoicing in foreign currency for the extension of credit or financing abroad; and
(f) capital authorization in rupiah.

[120] Foreign lenders wishing to take security over local immovable property are permitted to do so in Indonesia. This is regulated by Law No. 4 of 1996 on Security Rights over Land (commonly known as Hak Tanggungan) ('Law No. 4/1996') which states that the grant of Hak Tanggungan must be preceded by an agreement to give Hak Tanggungan a security for the repayment of the debt stated on the inseparable part of the loan agreement. Furthermore, in the elucidation of Law No. 4/1996, it is stated that the loan agreement can be made in Indonesia or outside Indonesia and that the related parties in the loan agreement can be a foreign individual or a foreign entity so long as such loan is used for development in the territory of Indonesia. The type of assets that can be encumbered by a security right over the land are immovable assets (land) and structures attached to the land, and the holder of the security right over the land must be an individual or a legal entity, which must be: (a) an Indonesian citizen; (b) a foreign citizen (domiciled or not domiciled in Indonesia); (c) an Indonesian legal entity; or (d) a foreign legal entity (having a representative office in Indonesia or headquartered overseas).

[121] In addition, there are controls over the transfer of funds to foreign lenders for the payment of interest or the repayment of capital which are classed as foreign exchange activities. BI Regulation No. 21/2/PBI/2019 concerning the Reporting of Foreign Exchange Traffic Activities requires that a foreign exchange traffic report must include: (a) the trading of goods, services, and other transactions between residents and foreign tax residents; (b) foreign debts and/or primary data concerning risk participation transactions; (c) foreign debts and/or withdrawal from risk participation transactions and/or payment plans for such withdrawal; (d) foreign debt and/or risk participation withdrawal and/or payment realization; (e) foreign financial assets, foreign financial liabilities, and/or risk participation transaction positions and amendments; and/or (f) new foreign debt obligations and/or their amendment. The report has to be submitted to BI by the parties carrying out the foreign exchange traffic activities, and if the report consists of data and information related to foreign debts and/or risk participation transactions, the relevant supporting documents must also be enclosed. Additionally, in entering into foreign debts, the parties must take account of BI Regulation No. 16/22/PBI/2014 concerning the Implementation of Prudential Principles in Offshore Loans Management by Non-Bank Corporations as last amended by BI Regulation No. 18/4/PBI/2016 of 2016.

2.6 M&A under the Company Law

2.6.1 Shareholder Approval

[122] Pursuant to the Company Law, merger transactions normally result in the merging company ceasing to exist by operation of law. The BoD of the company which is to merge and to survive the company is required to prepare a merger plan/proposal. Further, the merger plan must be submitted to the General Meeting of Shareholder (GMS) for approval after the BoC has given their approval. However, it should be noted that particular companies undertaking specific business activities (e.g., banks and non-bank financial institutions) wishing to merge need first to obtain approval from the related government agency in accordance with the relevant laws and regulations.

[123] Meanwhile, acquisition transactions must be conducted by the acquisition of shares that have been issued and/or will be issued by the company through the BoD of the company (initiated by the target company BoD) or by way of acquisition of existing shares (initiated by the shareholders). Both routes towards acquisition must be approved by a GMS resolution.

[124] According to the Company Law, a GMS to approve an M&A transaction may be held if at the meeting at least three-quarters of the total amount of shares having voting rights are present or represented, and the resolution can only be approved by at least three-fourths of the total amount of votes cast. Note that any PT's AoA may set a higher threshold for the quorum and for the votes required to pass the resolution.

[125] Furthermore, in the event shareholders do not approve the M&A transaction, shareholders have the right to request the company to buy their shares at an appropriate price, and such action does not prejudice or halt the merger or acquisition process.

[126] The GMS must be held at the company's domicile or at the company's principal place of business and, if the company is a public company, the GMS must be held at the domicile of the stock exchange where the company's shares are listed and must be located within the territory of the Republic of Indonesia. Apart from those provisions, the GMS may also be held via teleconference, video conference or other vehicles for electronic media.

2.6.2 Directors' Duties

Directors' Duties in Merger and Consolidation

[127] Mergers and Consolidations are two specific legal concepts under Company Law. A merger is defined as the legal act whereby a company merges with another existing company such that the assets and liabilities of the merging company transfer to the company that receives them, and the merging company ceases to exist by law.

[128] Consolidation is an action carried out by two or more companies that establish a new company, which by law receives the assets and liabilities of the consolidating companies and the consolidating companies cease to exist by law.

[129] In the case of a merger, the BoD must draw up a draft merger plan/proposal and submit that draft to the GMS of each company to obtain its approval, after obtaining the approval of the BoC of each company. Meanwhile, certain companies undertaking a merger may need approval from the relevant government agencies in accordance with prevailing laws and regulation. Furthermore, in the case of an acquisition, before completing the legal act of acquisition, the BoD must have approval from the GMS. The BoD of the company concerned must draw up a draft acquisition plan/proposal and obtain approval from the BoC.

[130] Furthermore, the BoD of the company which is to carry out the merger, consolidation, acquisition, or segregation (as the case may be) is also obliged to publish an abstract of the draft proposal for merger, consolidation, acquisition or segregation in at least one newspaper and must also publish it in writing to the employees of the company carrying it out no later than thirty days prior to calling the relevant GMS.

Directors' Duties in Acquisition

[131] The term 'acquisition' is a specific legal concept under the Company Law, defined as a 'legal act conducted by a person or a legal entity for the takeover of the shares of the (target) company that results in a change of control of such company'. The concept is thus distinguished from an ordinary share purchase that does not alter the control over the target company.

[132] The Company Law does not explicitly define what constitutes control. The control test is set out under sectoral regulations for companies whose business falls within the scope of the relevant regulations (e.g., capital market regulations for publicly listed companies, and banking and insurance regulations for banks and insurance business, respectively). For other companies to whom sectoral regulations do not apply, control is defined as a shareholder(s)' capacity to:

(a) appoint and dismiss members of the BoD or BoC, or
(b) to pass a resolution to amend the company's AoA.

[133] Furthermore, acquisition under the Company Law may take place either by way of the target company directors issuing new shares to be subscribed and paid for by the acquirer, or alternatively by direct purchase from the existing shareholders. Furthermore, the Company Law provides that an acquisition may be BoD-driven (i.e., by way of the BoD issuing new shares for the acquirer to subscribe and pay for) or shareholder-driven (i.e., by the sale of existing shares by the existing shareholders to the acquirer).

[134] For a BoD-driven acquisition, the boards of the target company and of the acquiring company must draw up a draft acquisition plan/proposal which needs to be approved by the BoC and the GMS. However, for an acquisition transaction which is conducted directly by shareholders, the directors do not need to prepare a plan of acquisition. Additionally, the directors need to take into account the provisions of the AoA of the acquired company and any agreements that have been made between the acquired company and other parties.

[135] Besides that, the directors are obliged to announce an abridged plan in at least 1 (one) newspaper and to announce in writing to the employees of the company that it is proposing to enter into an M&A transaction within thirty days prior to the call for a GMS. The announcement must contain a notification that interested parties may have access to the abridged plan of the M&A transaction at the office of the company from the date of announcement through to the date when the GMS is held. Creditors may submit an objection to the company within fourteen days after the announcement. Furthermore, in the event that the directors fail to meet the objection of the creditors until the GMS is held, this matter must be brought to the attention of the GMS meeting. If a resolution or settlement has not been reached in the course of the GMS, the M&A transaction must not be implemented.

[136] In addition, both the directors of the company surviving the merger as well as the directors of the acquired company must announce the consummation of the merger or acquisition in one or more newspaper(s) within thirty days of the date on which the merger or acquisition took effect.

[137] As regards 'hostile' transactions, the Company Law does not specifically regulate for situations where the target company's BoD resists the takeover.

2.6.3 Form of Consideration

[138] In general, shares are paid up in the form of money, but it is possible for shares to be paid up in some other form in accordance with the Company Law. The paying up of shares in a form other than money must be accompanied by a statement of the type or kind of the consideration, the value or the price attributed to it, and the relevant status and domicile of the party providing it, all as considered necessary for the sake of clarity. Furthermore a proper valuation process is required to determine the fair value of such consideration by reference to market prices, and if no market prices are available, the fair and reasonable value will be determined based on appraisal techniques most suitable to the characteristics of the payment, based on the best available relevant information, and undertaken by an independent expert who is not affiliated with the company. The payment-up of shares in exchange for immovable property must be announced in one or more newspapers within fourteen days after the signing of the deed of establishment or after the GMS has resolved on such payment-up. According to the Company Law, there is no restriction on the disposal of shares acquired as a result of shares being paid up in some form other than money.

2.6.4 Financial Assistance

[139] In general, there is no specific requirement affecting the ability of a company to provide a corporate guarantee. Guarantors arguably have an equal economic interest in the business with the borrower at least in the following circumstances:

(a) where the guarantor as a director and/or as a majority shareholder of the company, personally participates to guarantee the company's debt; or
(b) where a parent company guarantees the debt(s) of its subsidiaries.

[140] The company's AoA need to be reviewed to examine the circumstances in which the guarantor company might be debarred from making such a guarantee. Where no such provision exists, the purpose and business objective of the company need to be examined to see whether the guarantee is in line with such purpose and objective. Specifically, for the protection of shareholders in a public company, BAPEPAM Letter No. S-1505/PM/1997 on Corporate Guarantees provides that if a public company acts as a corporate guarantor for any of its subsidiaries, the public company must own 99.9% of the aggregate paid-up share capital of the subsidiary concerned.

[141] The company may obtain/provide financial assistance for the purchase of its own shares provided this is not in conflict with BI Regulation No. 8/2006. However, in terms of making such loans, the financial service sector must (pursuant to Indonesia OJK Regulation No. 23/POJK.01/2019 concerning the Amendment of Indonesia OJK Regulation No. 12/POJK.01/2017 regarding the Implementation of Anti-Money Laundering Program and Terrorism Financing Prevention in the Financial Services Sector ('OJK Regulation No. 23/2019') apply 'customer due diligence' and (if need be) 'enhanced due diligence' to the debtor to understand the identity of the debtor, and to monitor customer transactions including the reporting of suspicious transactions. Proof of solvency is not required since the bank normally applies such principles of its own volition.

[142] Customer due diligence (CDD) is an activity such as identification, verification and monitoring conducted by the bank in order to ensure that transactions are in line with the customer profile. Enhanced due diligence is a more comprehensive CDD conducted by the bank when dealing with high-risk customers (including politically exposed persons) or with the possibility of money laundering and/or the financing of terrorism.

2.6.5 Security Interests

[143] In principle the security available for bank loans depends on the type of object over which security is sought. These can be classified into the forms set out below:

(a) Immovable assets, for example, land and other objects inseparable from such land; which may be in the form of buildings, plant or machinery located on such land and which cannot be moved. This type of object can be encumbered with *Hak Tanggungan* under Law No. 4/1996;
(b) Movable assets, for example, cars, motorbikes, machines, accounts receivable, shares, etc which are commonly encumbered with three types of security – a fiduciary security, a pledge of shares, or a mortgage (for movable assets that weigh more than 20 m^3).
(c) An object that is built on some other party's property, for example, a building on land with a building exploitation permit.

[144] The distinction between fixed and floating charges familiar to Western jurisdictions is not provided for under Indonesian Law. However, Law No. 42 of 1999 on Fiduciary Security ('Law No. 42/1999') states in its explanation/elucidation that the objects of fiduciary securities may include movable assets, both tangible and intangible, and immovable assets which cannot be encumbered with *Hak Tanggungan*.

[145] There is a requirement to register most securities in Indonesia, even though not all guarantees are required to be registered. The securities that must be registered are as follows:

(a) Fiduciary securities, by signing a notarial deed before an Indonesian notary and registration by an online mechanism in accordance with Directorate General of Public Administration Circular Letter No. AHU-06.OT.03.01/2013 Jo. Article 14(1) and Article 16(2) Law No. 42/1999. As evidence of registration, the applicant will receive a registration statement, which can be downloaded from the website. The type of assets covered by this form of security are movable (intangible or tangible) assets and immovable assets, especially buildings which cannot be encumbered with Security Rights over land as referred to in Law No. 4/1996. These remain under the control of the provider of the fiduciary security, as collateral for the repayment of debt, and afford priority to the recipient's debt as against other creditors.
(b) Security Rights over Land: by signing a *hak tanggungan* deed before a Land Deed Official (commonly known as '*Pejabat Pembuat Akta Tanah*') and registering such deed at the Land Office. Upon such registration in the *hak tanggungan* land book, *hak tanggungan* will be perfected. A certificate provides evidence of registration.
(c) Security right over warehouse receipt: this is effected by signing a deed of security agreement, notifying the Registration Centre (PT *Kliring Berjangka Indonesia*) and the warehouse manager, annotating the right in/at the Registry Book of Security, and obtaining confirmation of the notification.

[146] In the event of insolvency, according to Article 1134 of the Indonesia Civil Code, pledges and mortgages are superior to privileges, unless stipulated otherwise by the law. In Article 95 paragraph 4 Law No. 13 of 2003 on Manpower ('Law No. 13/2003') as amended by Law No. 11/2020 it is stated that in the event of bankruptcy or liquidation as referred to in prevailing laws, employees have priority rights to payment in respect of their wages or other rights. The payment of unpaid wages of employees is prioritized before the payment to all other creditors, while the payment of other rights of employees takes precedence over all creditors other than creditors holding collateral rights. This priority is based on Article 138 of Law No. 37 of 2004 on Bankruptcy and Postponement of Debt Settlement Obligations ('Law No. 37/2004').

[147] Furthermore, the 'suspect period' is defined as the period running from the date on which the debtor ceases payments. Any transactions undertaken by the debtor in this period may be declared void. If they were undertaken in exchange for payment, proof would be needed that the persons contracting with the debtor were aware that the latter had ceased payments. In Indonesia, according to Law No. 37/2004 a distinction is drawn between insolvency and bankruptcy. Insolvency occurs if, following the declaration of a company's bankruptcy by the court:

(a) no composition plan is submitted by the company to its creditors; or
(b) a composition plan is submitted but is subsequently rejected by its creditors; or
(c) a composition plan is submitted and is subsequently approved by the creditors but is not ratified by the court.

[148] A company may be pronounced bankrupt by the court if the following tests are fulfilled:

(a) the company has at least two creditors (the so-called plurality of creditors test); and
(b) at least one of the two debts is currently due and payable.

[149] After a company has been declared bankrupt by the court, the debtor company cannot conduct any further transactions. Nevertheless, prior to the declaration of bankruptcy any creditor, public prosecutor, BI, or OJK may apply to the court to:

(a) authorize seizure (pursuant to a security) of all or any part of the debtor's assets; or
(b) appoint a temporary receiver to control the management of the debtor's business and to pay the creditor(s).

[150] This application may be granted if it is intended to protect the interests of the creditor. Additionally, to file for insolvency of any company, reference needs to be made to the new technical guidelines stated in the Guidelines Book on Bankruptcy and Postponement of Debt Settlement Obligations. This was required following the Decision of Supreme Court No. 109/KMA/SK/IV/2020 on implementation of the Guidelines Book on Bankruptcy and Postponement of Debt Settlement Obligations.

2.6.6 Completion Formalities

[151] The formalities required in order to effect the transfer of shares, land or other assets include, among others:

(a) For the transfer of shares pursuant to a merger or acquisition transaction, rights over shares must be transferred by the execution of a deed of transfer of rights. The deed of transfer of rights (or a copy thereof) must then be submitted to the company in writing, and the BoD must record the transfer of rights over shares in the register of shareholders/special register and announce the amendment of the company's shareholding structure to the Ministry of Law and Human Rights (MOLHR) at least thirty days from the registration of the transfer of rights in the Company Registry. For merger or acquisition transactions within specific regulated sectors, the parties must comply with the regulatory provisions of the relevant governmental agency.

For instance, the financial sector needs to comply with Indonesia OJK regulations.

(b) For the effective transfer of land, transfers must (in accordance with Government Regulation No. 18 of 2021 on Management Rights, Land Rights, Apartment Units and Land Registration jo. Law No. 5 of 1960 on Basic Provision on Agrarian Principles) be effected by means of sale and purchase, exchange, grant, inclusion in the company, and other legal acts that transfer rights. The requirements to effect such transactions include a deed of transfer made by a Land Deed Official (*Pejabat Pembuat Akta Tanah* or PPAT); following which the deed of transfer must be listed in the Land Book in the Land Registry Office, after which a certificate of ownership of the relevant land will be issued by the Land Registry Office. On 2021 the enforcement of electronic land title certificates will be implemented, where proof of ownership of a land certificate or land book will no longer be made of paper, but rather an electronic land certificate whose data is included in the land system and this is further stipulated in the Regulation of the Minister of ATR/Head of BPN No. 1 of 2021 on Electronic Certificates.

[152] In Indonesia, the most important thing, in terms of transfer formalities, is the method of transfer (*levering*). Transfers are divided into two forms – the transfer of a movable asset, which in turn is divided into the transfer of a tangible movable asset and the transfer of an intangible movable asset, and the transfer of an immovable asset. The transfer of intangible movable assets is effected by hand to hand delivery, which means that the factual transfer and the juridical transfer are conducted simultaneously. On the other hand, for the transfer of an immovable asset, the factual transfer and the juridical transfer are conducted at different times. A transfer of an immovable asset is not only conducted through factual transfer but is also recorded in a transfer letter (*'akte van transport'*) which is subsequently registered.

2.6.7 Costs and Fees

[153] The main costs and fees arising in relation to merger and acquisition transactions are notary fees; obtaining approvals for amendments to the AoA; announcements required by the Company Law; and related government fees and taxes. Generally, no government fees are charged for processing government approvals for merger and acquisition transactions.

[154] Necessary filings, disclosures, notifications, announcements or completion certificates are all stipulated under the Company Law. Therefore, under the Law, before conducting a merger transaction the BoD must draft a plan/proposal for the merger which comprises:

(a) The name and domicile of each company involved in the merger.
(b) The reasons and explanations of the BoD of the companies involved in the merger, and the merger requirements.

(c) The procedures for valuation and for the conversion of shares in the merging company into shares of the surviving company.
(d) A draft of any amendment of the AoA of the surviving company.
(e) A financial report covering the last three financial years for each of the companies involved in the merger.
(f) The plans for continuing or terminating the business activities of the company in the merger.
(g) A pro forma balance sheet of the surviving company in accordance with accounting principles generally applied in Indonesia.
(h) The method of resolution of the status, rights and obligations of the members of the BoD, the BoC and employees of the merging company.
(i) The method of resolution of the rights and obligations of the merging company as against third parties.
(j) The method of resolution of the rights of shareholders who do not agree to the merger of the company.
(k) The names of the members of the BoD and BoC of the surviving company and their wages, honoraria, and allowances.
(l) The estimated period required for implementation of the merger.
(m) A report on the circumstances, development and results achieved of each of the companies involved in the merger.
(n) The main activities of each company involved in the merger and any changes which occurred in the current financial year.
(o) Details of any problems arising during the current financial year which affected the activities of the companies involved in the merger.

[155] As mentioned above, in relation to directors' duties, the summary of such a plan/proposal must be published in at least one newspaper and must be announced in writing to the employees of the company planning to implement the merger. After obtaining approval from the GMS, the merger plan must be drawn up in a deed of merger before a notary in Bahasa Indonesia to which must be attached on the application to obtain approval of the MOLHR and the delivery notification to the MOLHR of the amendment of the AoA. If the merger is not accompanied by an amendment of the AoA, a copy of the deed of merger must be delivered to MOLHR to be recorded in the register of the company.

[156] There are certain disclosure requirements pursuant to Article 127 paragraph 2 of the Company Law. The BoD of the company entering into an acquisition must make an announcement of the summary plan to the public through at least one newspaper. The summary plan of the acquisition must include at least:

(a) The name and domicile of the acquiring company and of the company to be acquired.
(b) The reasons and explanations of the BoD of the acquiring company and of the company to be acquired.
(c) The financial reports for the most recent fiscal year of the acquiring company and of the company to be acquired.

(d) The procedures for valuation and conversion of shares of the company to be acquired into shares of the acquiring company (if payment for the acquisition is to be made in shares).
(e) The number of shares to be acquired.
(f) Intentions/plans for funding the acquisition.
(g) A pro forma consolidated balance sheet of the acquiring company after the acquisition compiled in accordance with accounting principles generally applied in Indonesia.
(h) Proposed method of resolution of rights of shareholders who do not agree with the acquisition.
(i) Proposed method of resolution of the status, rights and obligations of members of the BoD, the BoC, and employees of the company to be acquired.
(j) Estimate of the period required for implementation of the acquisition, including the period for the grant to the company's BoD of powers of attorney from the shareholders to assign their shares.
(k) A draft of any amendment of the AoA of the company resulting from the acquisition.

[157] If an acquisition of shares is conducted directly by the shareholders, the summary of the above details does not apply. However, there are disclosure requirements set out in Law No. 40/2007 as amended by Law No. 11/2020, pursuant to which the BoD of the company entering into an acquisition must announce the abridged plan to the public through at least one newspaper. Upon completion of the acquisition, the BoD is required to disclose the acquisition by announcing it in a newspaper not later than thirty days from the effective date of the acquisition.

[158] If the merger or acquisition transaction involves foreign capital investment (PMA) or domestic capital investment (PMDN) companies, a report must be submitted to the OSS System for any relevant sectoral ministries, agencies and/or regional government authorities for purposes of monitoring/supervision in accordance with applicable relevant laws and regulations. Additionally, a PMA will need to consider the positive list for investment to ensure that it can carry out the intended transaction.

[159] In addition, disclosure is also required to be made to KPPU for any merger or acquisition which results in aggregate assets exceeding IDR2.5 trillion or aggregate revenues exceeding IDR5 trillion. If two or more parties involved in the acquisition are companies engaging in the business of banking, disclosure is required if the acquisition results in aggregate assets of more than IDR20 trillion.

[160] For public company acquisitions, both parties must consider the percentage of shares held, since (according to the OJK Regulation No. 11/POJK.04/2017 on the Reporting of Substantial Shareholdings in Public Company) there is an obligation to report substantial shareholdings, as well as any change of shareholding of 0.5% or more by any shareholder who directly or indirectly holds 5% or more of the total issued shares in a public company. And, simply stated, the ultimate beneficial owners are now required to report their shareholdings.

2.6.8 Dividends

[161] The only source of dividends that the Company Law recognizes is distributable profit. Company profits may be distributed as dividends only if the following conditions are met:

(a) The company books net profits in the relevant financial year.
(b) The net profit in that financial year exceeds any cumulative losses sustained in previous years.
(c) The company has a reserve amounting to at least 20% of its subscribed and paid-up capital.
(d) The GMS has not passed a resolution to allocate or expend profits of the company in some different manner.

[162] The Company Law does not discriminate between foreign or domestic shareholders. Shares entitle their owners to, among others, receive dividends, and this right is contingent upon ownership of such shares and not the nationality of the owners. Meanwhile, the Investment Law states that investors are permitted to transfer and repatriate their dividends However, this needs to be done in compliance with the related prevailing law and regulations. Currently, such transfers must be conducted in the form of rupiah.

[163] As regards taxation, there are differences in treatment between domestic shareholders and foreign shareholders. These differences are as follows:

(a) Dividends paid to resident taxpayer recipients are subject to Article 23 involving income tax withholding at 15% from gross earnings.
(b) Dividends paid to non-resident recipients are subject to 20% (lower for treaty countries) final withholding tax on dividends.
(c) Dividends paid to individual taxpayers are subject to Article 4 paragraph (2) income tax withholding at 10% from gross earnings.

[164] The issue of reserves is relevant here. The Company Law recognizes two kinds of reserves: Mandatory Reserves and Other Reserves. The Mandatory Reserve is intended to cover the possibility of future losses. Its use is restricted to cover losses that other reserves cannot cover. A Mandatory Reserve does not have to be in cash. However it has to be adequately liquid and it cannot be distributed by way of dividends. While Other Reserves are reserves excluding the Mandatory Reserves, which can be used for various purposes of the company such as business expansion, dividends, social and other purposes.

[165] Generally, every company must set aside money from net profits (profit after tax) for the establishment and maintenance of a Mandatory Reserve. The amount of the Mandatory Reserve is 20% of the paid-up capital. The obligation to form and set up such Mandatory Reserve arises only where the company books net profit more than covering any losses sustained in the previous year. Note, however, that dividends may not be paid out to the shareholders until both previous years' losses have been covered and the 20% Mandatory Reserve requirement has been met.

2.6.9 Purchase of Own Shares

[166] In accordance with Article 37 of Law No. 40/2007 as amended by Law No. 11/2020, the repurchase by a company of its own shares must not cause the net assets of the company to reduce below the level of the company's issued capital plus allocated mandatory reserves. In the event of repurchase of shares by the company any pledge of shares or fiduciary securities over shares held by the company itself or by some other company whose shares are directly or indirectly owned by the company must not exceed 10% of the total amount of issued capital in the company unless otherwise provided by legislative regulation in the capital market sector. Following repurchase, the bought back shares may be held by the company for not more than three years. These restrictions are intended to allow time for the company to determine whether the shares will be sold or withdrawn through a reduction in capital. In order to be able to carry out a buyback of shares it is necessary to consider the equilibrium repurchase price (ERP) of the bought back shares.

2.6.10 The Corporate Veil

[167] There are two ways in which a parent company can become liable for the debts or other liabilities of its subsidiaries under Indonesian Law. First, by guaranteeing the obligations of the subsidiary and, second, if it meets one of the criteria listed under Article 3(2) of the Company Law.

[168] A parent company's guarantee may set aside the corporate veil and may render the parent company liable for the obligations of its subsidiary. The guarantee under Indonesian Law is an agreement, made for the benefit of an obligor, under which a third party binds itself to fulfil the obligations of the obligor where such obligor fails to fulfil the obligations itself. The law makes no distinction between whether the guarantor is a parent company or a natural person, a shareholder or an independent third person.

[169] With respect to Article 3 paragraph 2 of Law No. 40/2007 as amended by Law No. 11/2020, the law provides that the parent company may become personally liable if one of these criteria is met:

(a) The requirements for the company as a legal entity have not or are no longer being fulfilled.
(b) The relevant shareholder directly or indirectly and in bad faith exploits the company for its/his own interests.
(c) The relevant shareholder is involved in an action contrary to the law committed by the company.
(d) The relevant shareholder directly or indirectly and in contravention of the law utilizes the company's assets, which results in the assets of the company becoming insufficient to satisfy the company's debts.

[170] Another significant issue concerning this 'lifting of the corporate veil' is the individual directors' and commissioners' liabilities. In the event of bankruptcy caused by fault on the part of the BoC or by negligence in supervising the BoD' management of the company and where the company's assets are insufficient to pay all of the company's liabilities, every member of the BoD and of the BoC are personally and jointly and severally liable to settle the company's outstanding debts.

2.6.11 Insolvency

[171] The main implications of buying shares or businesses which have gone into insolvency are that, if after buying shares, the investor becomes a majority shareholder, then the investor must manage the interests of all creditors as well as all the debts of the company. Before an investor buys shares of a target company that has gone into insolvency, it is necessary to consider the interests of the minority shareholders of the company, the company's employees, creditors, and other business partners, as well as the public and issues of fair business competition.

[172] On buying shares or a business that has gone into insolvency, there are special considerations that may arise in relation to the status of the company – in particular whether the company will be dissolved or will continue its business.

Dissolution of Bankrupt Company

[173] After being declared bankrupt, a company is not automatically dissolved. The dissolution of a company after completion of the bankruptcy process depends on the Judge's Decision in response to the request for dissolution. According to Article 142 of Law No. 40/2007 as amended by Law No. 11/2020, there are two reasons for company dissolution which are related to bankruptcy, namely:

(a) By the revocation of bankruptcy under a Commercial Court Decision having binding legal force, the bankruptcy assets are insufficient to pay the bankruptcy costs.
(b) Because the bankruptcy assets of a company which has been declared bankrupt are in a state of insolvency as provided in the Bankruptcy and Postponement of Debt Settlement Obligation Law.

[174] Furthermore, Article 18 paragraph (1) Law No. 37/2004 provides that if a company is bankrupt such that it cannot afford to pay its debts, a creditor may make an application to the Supervising Judge for the company's dissolution based on the bankruptcy statement submitted by the debtor. Based on such creditor request, the Supervising Judge will propose to the Commercial Court, and after validly summoning or hearing the debtor, the Supervising Judge may decide to revoke the decision of bankruptcy. Based on the decision of the Commercial Court, a company may be dissolved. The dissolution of a company is followed by a settlement enabling the creditor to obtain repayment from such settlement.

The Company Still Continues Its Business

[175] Not every company that has been through a bankruptcy process will be dissolved. Pursuant to the explanation/elucidation of Law No. 37/2004, there is a

Business Continuity Principle in Law No. 37/2004 which allows a Debtor Company to continue its business if it has reasonable prospects of doing so successfully; this principle provides that as a matter of law the fact of bankruptcy does not in itself force the company to dissolve. Pursuant to Article 104 paragraph (1) of Law No. 37/2004, the business continuity of a bankrupt company depends on the approval of Creditor Committee as to the business prospects of the bankrupt debtor in the future. By considering Article 104 paragraph (1) of Law No. 37/2004 and the Business Continuity Principle, the Curator, along with the Creditor Committee may, subject to the approval of the Supervisory Judge, propose that a company which has been declared bankrupt and insolvent may nevertheless continue to operate its business. In addition, to file for insolvency of a company, reference must be made to the new technical guidelines as stated in the Guidelines Book on Bankruptcy and Postponement of Debt Settlement Obligations, which was required by the Decision of Supreme Court No. 109/KMA/SK/IV/2020 concerning the implementation of the Guidelines Book on Bankruptcy and Postponement of Debt Settlement Obligations.

[176] Buying shares of a company that has gone into insolvency and has been dissolved is not possible. Buying shares of a company that has gone into insolvency but still continues to operate its business is possible, but there are many factors which a buyer would need to weigh up, including, most importantly, whether the company is likely to be able to continue its business and to earn a profit.

2.6.12 Choice of Law

[177] There is no specific regulation concerning the choice of law in Indonesia; choice of law is recognized in Indonesia based on the doctrines of *lex loci contractus* (law of the place where the contract is made), *lex loci solutionis* (law of the place where the relevant performance occurs), and the proper law of the contract based on its most characteristic connection. At the same time, the principal source of the law of arbitration in Indonesia is Law No. 30 of 1999 on Arbitration and Alternative Dispute Resolution ('Law No. 30/1999'). According to Law No. 30/1999, a dispute is arbitrable only if that dispute is of a commercial nature (i.e., commerce, banking, finance, capital investment, and industry) and concerns rights which, as a matter of law and regulation, fall within the full legal authority of the disputing parties. In addition, arbitration is not permitted for a matter which, as a matter of law, cannot be settled privately.

[178] Moreover, a written arbitration agreement obviates the rights of the parties to bring a dispute in the district courts, which would otherwise have jurisdiction over a civil dispute. The district courts have no authority to hear disputes where parties are bound by an arbitration agreement, and they are required to reject and not to participate in the resolution of disputes which have already been adjudicated by arbitration, except in limited circumstances as provided in Law No. 30/1999.

[179] International Arbitration Awards will only be recognized and enforced in the jurisdiction of the Republic of Indonesia if they fulfil the following criteria:

(1) the International Arbitration Award is rendered by an arbitrator or arbitration panel in a country which is bound to the Republic of Indonesia by a bilateral or multilateral treaty on the recognition and enforcement of International Arbitration Awards;
(2) International Arbitration Awards, to be enforceable in Indonesia, are limited to awards which fall within the scope of commercial law under Indonesian law;
(3) International Arbitration Awards, to be enforceable in Indonesia, are limited to those which do not conflict with public order;
(4) an International Arbitration Award may be enforced in Indonesia after obtaining a writ of execution from the Chairman of the Central Jakarta District Court; and
(5) International Arbitration Awards, which involve the State of the Republic of Indonesia as one of the parties to the dispute, may only be enforced after obtaining an exequatur from the Supreme Court of the Republic of Indonesia, which will then delegate it to the Central Jakarta District Court.

[180] According to the principle of freedom of contract, the parties may conclude an agreement based on the consent of the parties as long as it satisfies the following conditions: (a) there must be a consent of the individuals who are bound thereby; (b) the parties must have the capacity to conclude an agreement; (c) there must be a specific subject; (d) there must be an admissible cause. Thus a contractual agreement which is subject to the law of a different jurisdiction may be recognized as long as it fulfils these requirements.

2.7 M&A for Public Companies

[181] The basic regulations governing M&A in Indonesia are the Company Law and Government Regulation No. 27 of 1998 on Merger, Consolidation, and Acquisition of a Limited Liability Company ('GR No. 27/1998'). Law No. 8 of 1995 on the Capital Market enables special regulations on mergers and acquisitions to be issued by regulating bodies for public companies. Since 2013, the competent authority regulating public takeovers on the capital market is the Indonesia OJK (previously the Capital Market and Financial Institution Supervisory Agency (BAPEPAM-LK)). Although BAPEPAM-LK was replaced by the OJK, all prevailing BAPEPAM-LK regulations remain in force until replaced or revoked. For public companies, there are specific regulations, including:

(a) OJK Regulation No. 9/POJK.04/2018 on the Acquisition of Public Companies;
(b) OJK Regulation No. 74/POJK.04/2016 on the Merger or Consolidation of Public Companies;
(c) OJK Regulation No. 54/POJK.04/2015 on Voluntary Tender Offers; and
(d) OJK Regulation No. 58/POJK.04/2017 on the Electronic Submission of Registration Statements and Applications for Corporate Actions.

[182] These rules referred to above are applicable to all public companies listed on the Indonesia Stock Exchange (IDX). The most common method of acquiring a public company in Indonesia is by direct acquisition of the existing shares from the shareholders. But apart from this most common method, there may be an indirect form of acquisition in which the BoD is involved, and by which investors can acquire a shareholding, such as:

(a) Debt-to-equity swap

By carrying out a debt-to-equity swap, the target company benefits from a boost to cash flow resulting from the reduction or elimination of ongoing repayments of principal and interest costs. However, this may disadvantage existing shareholders of the target company, given that the equity used in the debt-to-equity swap originates from the portfolio capital of the target company, thus diluting the percentage of an existing shareholder's interest (their shares decline in value).

(b) Private placement

The advantages of a private placement are:

(i) The procedure is faster and more cost effective. This is because the target company may offer the shares without registration with the OJK.
(ii) The target company is free to choose its investors, as the private placement is only offered to a limited number of investors.

The disadvantage of a private placement may be the difficulty of finding suitable investors. This is because the offer does not involve registration with the OJK, as a result of which there is no announcement of the offering. This can lead to the target company facing difficulty in finding suitable investors.

(c) Rights issue

The advantage of a rights issue is that the shares offered in a right issue are usually at a cheaper price than the existing shares. However, this may be a disadvantage for shareholders not taking up the offer (using their pre-emptive right to do so), because their shares may become diluted.

[183] The responsibilities of a director of a target company, on receiving a takeover offer, are as follows:

(a) In taking any action, the directors must comply with the interests, objective and purpose of the target company (Fiduciary Duty/Article 92(1) Law No. 40/2007).
(b) The directors must notify the offer to the shareholders of the target company.

[184] If the acquisition is carried out through the target company's directors, they may decline the acquisition offer from the directors of the acquiring company. However, if the acquisition is carried out directly through the shareholders, the directors do not have any basis or ability to resist the change of control.

[185] It is also possible for a buyer to make a partial offer. As mentioned before on the takeover structure, the acquiring company may make a partial offer to the target company to buy only some (not all) of their shares. If this results in a majority of the shares becoming controlled by the acquiring company, the transaction will be considered as an acquisition. This partial offer may be performed by means of a 'voluntary' bid through the stock exchange by the company (OJK Regulation No. 54/POJK.04/2015). In circumstances where the acquirer is unable to approach the targeted company outside the stock exchange, it may be possible for it to make a partial offer for shares of the targeted company through the stock exchange.

[186] Mandatory Tender Offers (MTOs) are regulated under OJK Regulation No. 9/POJK.04/2018. MTOs are applicable to situations where, after acquiring a certain level of shares of a public listed company by deed of acquisition, the new controlling company is obliged to hold a tender offer for the remaining shares of the acquired company. The obligation to make an MTO is triggered when the new controlling company acquires 80% of the issued shares of the acquired company, at which point the controlling company is required to make an MTO for the remaining 20% of shares of the acquired company owned by the public. In addition, the MTO gives rights to the shareholders of the acquired company to sell their shares to the public through the bid. The applicable regulations on the purchase of shares in advance of or during a bid are as follows:

(a) OJK Regulation 14/POJK.04/2019 regarding the Amendment to Regulation of the OJK No. 32/POJK.04/2015 regarding Capital Increases of Public Companies with Pre-emptive Rights (*Hak Memesan Efek Terlebih Dahulu*). This regulation governs the pre-emptive right (e.g., in terms of any rights issue) of existing shareholders to maintain their existing percentage ownership on any capital increases of a public company. This pre-emptive right is afforded to the existing shareholders in order to buy shares in advance of the rights issue. It is intended to prevent the shares of existing shareholders from being diluted and for the protection of minority shareholders.
(b) OJK Regulation No. 54/POJK.04/2015 on the Voluntary Tender Offer. This regulation governs the making of voluntary tender offers for the purpose of acquiring a target company. It is performed by the acquiring company in circumstances where it may be unaware of the identity of the target company's shareholders. Thus the acquiring company may carry out the offer/bid through the stock exchange in order to ascertain the shareholders of the target company's shares.
(c) OJK Regulation No. 9/POJK.04/2018 on the Acquisition of Public Company. This regulation governs the procedure required to carry out the acquisition of a public company through the capital market. There are several actions that must be carried out by an acquiring company, one of these being the mandatory bid, which is intended to maintain 20% of the shares of the target company being owned by the public.
(d) OJK Regulation No. 11/POJK.04/2017 on the Reporting of Substantial Shareholdings in Public Company. This regulation obliges the director or the

commissioner of a listed company/public company to report the ownership of the shares to OJK if there is a transaction in the shares.

(e) BAPEPAM Regulation No. IX.E.1: Annex of the Decision of the Head of BAPEPAM No. KEP-412/BL/2009 on Affiliated Transactions and Conflict of Interest Transactions. This regulation is intended to give legal certainty and protection for the shareholders, especially the independent shareholders, in relation to transactions carried out by a listed company or a public company with affiliated persons or where a conflict of interest arises. The protection is afforded by requiring a public announcement of the affiliated transaction.

(f) OJK Regulation No. 17/POJK.04/2020 on Material Transactions and Changes of Business Activity. This regulation governs 'material transactions', meaning transactions involving an amount equal to 20% or more of the equity of the public company (but if the public company has negative equity, the relevant calculation for the transaction is equal to 10% or more of the total assets of the public company). If the acquisition is for a majority of the shares of a target company (e.g., through a voluntary bid), it will automatically be considered as a material transaction. In these circumstances, there are a number of specific actions which must be undertaken by the acquiring company, pursuant to the regulation, before it is able to implement the transaction.

[187] In relation to obligations regarding announcement/disclosure associated with such share purchases, the director or commissioner of the issuer or public company must (according to OJK Regulation No. 11/POJK.04/2017) report to the OJK on the ownership and every change of ownership of shares of his company, within ten days after the execution of the transaction. This obligation also applies to every party owning 5% or more of the company's issued share capital. A copy of the required report must be made available by the OJK for public disclosure.

[188] A target company can offer exclusivity or a break fee where this is agreed between the parties, and it is not regulated under the prevailing laws and regulations. In the context of a private acquisition, the exclusivity may be given by the target company to the buyer before drafting the Share Purchase Agreement (PJBS/*Perjanjian Jual Beli Saham*). The commitment of the target company may be obtained by stating the exclusivity in the preliminary Memorandum of Understanding agreed between the parties.

[189] Specific difficulties and constraints arising on normal due diligence include, among other things, that the relevant documents are incomplete, that the relevant permits may already have expired, and that the target company may not have disclosed several of the required documents. Basically, due diligence is normally feasible in the context of a public takeover, including legal due diligence, operational due diligence and financial due diligence. According to OJK Regulation No. 9/POJK.04/2018 on Acquisition of Public Company, an acquirer is permitted to publicly disclose information about ongoing negotiations with selling shareholders or to keep the information confidential. The following are the minimum components that must be included in the disclosure obligation:

- Estimates of the number of shares that will be acquired.
- The identity of the acquirer (name, address, telephone number, types of business activity and the purpose of the takeover).
- The number of securities already owned by the acquirer (if any).
- Plan or decision to co-operate between parties acting in concert in an organized group for the purpose of the takeover (if any).
- Method and process of the negotiation.
- Content of the negotiation.

[190] Information that must be disclosed following completion of the takeover includes:

- The number of shares acquired and the total ownership of shares.
- The identity of the parties (name, address, telephone number, types of business activity and the purpose of the takeover).
- Statement that the acquirer is an organized group, if that is the case.

[191] In addition, according to OJK Regulation No. 11/POJK.04/2017 on the Reporting of Substantial Shareholdings in a Public Company, a person who acquires, either directly or indirectly, an interest of 5% or more of a public listed company (specifically the ultimate beneficial owner) is obliged to disclose this interest to the OJK. This publicly available information must be in the form of a report consisting of Indonesia–53(i) name, domicile, and nationality; (ii) name of the public company; (iii) the number of shares and the ownership percentage both before and after the relevant transactions; (iv) the number of shares purchased or sold; (v) the purchase and sale price of each of the shares; (vi) the date of the transaction; (vii) the purpose/object of the transaction; (viii) the ownership status (direct or indirect); (ix) the identity of the ultimate beneficial owner and also of the shareholder actually registered in the shareholder's register of the public company on behalf of the ultimate beneficial owner.

[192] If there are undisclosed liabilities in the target company, the buyer may protect himself, through the confidentiality agreement executed prior to commencement of the due diligence, by clearly stating the obligation of both parties to disclose every required document. If the confidentiality agreement is violated, it is then possible for the buyer to sue the public company through the courts.

[193] There are certain rules applied to information leaking out in advance of a bid. This may be considered as an 'insider trading' crime in the capital market. According to Article 95 of Law No. 8/1995 on the Capital Market, an 'insider' of the issuer or of the public company which has the relevant information must not purchase or sell any securities of the relevant issuer or public company, or of any other company undertaking a transaction with that issuer or public company. The following individuals will be considered as 'insiders' with respect to insider trading:

- Commissioners, directors or employees of a public company.
- The principal shareholder(s) of a public company.
- Individuals who, due to their position, profession or business relationship with a listed or public company, are able to obtain inside information.

- Parties who, within the last six months prior to the relevant date, fell into one of the above categories.

[194] It is possible to offer securities as consideration for public takeovers in lieu of cash. There are several securities that may be offered to the seller in this context, including:

(a) Shares, which are:
  (i) Share contribution (*Inbreng Saham*)
  This method is carried out by transferring shares of a subsidiary of the acquiring company by way of payment. Following implementation of the share contribution, the target company becomes the shareholder of the acquiring company's subsidiary.
  (ii) Share swap
  This method is a share exchange between one company and another company. In this method, the exchanged shares originate from the portfolio of the company issuing shares for the purpose of the share swap. After the share swap transaction, each of the companies has shares previously owned by the other.
  (iii) Shareholders' share exchange
  This method is the exchange of shares that have been paid up and subscribed by the shareholders.

(b) Bonds
Payment may be made in corporate bonds in the context of a so-called Combination Based Acquisition, where the payment is made through a combination of shares, bonds, and other assets.

[195] In the context of a public takeover it is not mandatory for the same terms to be offered to all the shareholders. This is because individual shareholders may wish to exercise a preference in terms of the consideration offered. In order to pay for the acquired company, the acquiring company may use a combination of different payment methods, and this is regarded as a combination acquisition.

[196] In Indonesia, there is also no obligation on the acquiring company to acquire other classes of security in the target company. However, there are several options or convertible securities that may be offered by the target company to be acquired by the acquiring company, which are:

(a) Assets
The acquiring company may acquire the undertaking and assets of the target company. These assets may provide security for bonds regarded as debt securities.

(b) Convertible bonds
These are a form of security which may be relevant in the context of a gradual acquisition, where the target company offers convertible bonds (bonds that may be converted into shares) for purchase by the acquiring company. In the first phase of this process, the acquiring company provides funds

to the target company in order to buy its convertible bonds. Then, in the second phase, the bonds in question may be converted into shares of the target company, generally where the performance of the target company is improving.

[197] Generally speaking, in the acquisition process, no assessment is carried out by OJK on the financial ability of the acquiring company to acquire the target company. Nor does OJK impose any conditions on the amount of finance required. However, in the context of an MTO (where the acquiring company is obliged to offer to buy the remaining shares), the acquiring company must provide proof stating that the new controller has sufficient funds and must offer full disclosure on the sources of funding.

[198] As regards the timetable, there is a control issue that can affect the timetable of a public takeover, namely that companies must submit a notification to the Indonesian Business Competition Supervisory Commission (KPPU) of any takeover which could result in a monopoly or unfair business competition (as determined by the specific thresholds set out in Government Regulation No. 57 of 2010 on Mergers or Consolidations of Business Entities and Acquisitions of Companies' Shares Which May Result in Monopolistic Practices or Unfair Business Competition (GR No. 57/2010) (*see* below for further information).

[199] In the case of an acquisition transaction, the documents that should be reviewed by the regulators are:

(a) Submission to the Minister of Law and Human Rights of the announcement and of a copy of the acquisition deed (attached to the submission of the announcement).
(b) After control of the target company has been acquired, the success of the transaction is assumed. Thus the new controlling company must announce the acquisition to the public and to the OJK, within one working day after the acquisition of control. The information to be disclosed must include:
  (i) The number/amount of shares acquired and the new aggregate total of shares owned.
  (ii) The personal identity of the acquiring and acquired company.
  (iii) The purpose of acquiring control.
  (iv) Statement (if it is the case) that the new controlling entity is an organized group/concert party group.
  (v) The ultimate beneficial owner of the party carrying out the takeover transaction, if that party is not itself the ultimate beneficial owner.
  (v) The nature of any affiliation with a public company, if there is an affiliate relationship.
  (vi) A description of any approval obtained by an authorized party, if any such approval was required.
(c) To carry out an MTO, the controlling company must:
  (i) Submit a text of the announcement containing the required disclosures and the relevant supporting documents to the OJK. The announcement must include:

- The background of the acquisition.
- Information on the shares.
- Information on the new controller.
- Information on the acquired company.
- Any contract or activities which have a material impact.
- The terms and conditions of the MTO.
- The list of names and addresses of the Capital Market Support Institution and/or professional advisers involved in the MTO.
- Other material information.

(ii) After the MTO has been carried out, the controlling company must submit a report on the result to the OJK.

[200] In the case of a merger transaction, the relevant requirements are:

(1) Names, domiciles, business activities, capital structures and shareholders of any merging or consolidating companies, as well as details regarding their management and supervisory structures.
(2) Name, domicile, the BoD and BoC composition of the surviving company (for mergers) or of the new company (for consolidations).
(3) Reasons for and timetable/schedule for the intended merger or consolidation.
(4) Procedures for the conversion of the merging/consolidating companies' shares to shares of the surviving/new company.
(5) Draft amendment of the surviving company's AoA (if any) or draft of the new company's deed of establishment.
(6) A summary of essential financial data derived from the merging/consolidating companies' audited financial statements for (a) the last two years (if the companies are public companies); or (b) three years (for any private companies which are also participating in the merger/consolidation).
(7) A comparison of financial data from the current interim period with data from the last accounting year's interim period (if any).
(8) Pro forma financial information for the surviving/new company, duly reviewed by public accountants.
(9) A summary of an assessor's report on (a) the share value attributable to each of the merging/consolidating companies; and (b) the fairness of the merger or consolidation
(10) The results of an expert assessment of certain aspects of the merger/consolidation (if deemed necessary)
(11) A legal opinion regarding the merger/consolidation
(12) Procedures to be followed by the merging or consolidating companies when resolving any of the following matters:
    (a) status of their employees;
    (b) rights and obligations of any third parties; and
    (c) rights of shareholders that may conflict with the merger or consolidation.

(13) Description of the various benefits and risks which may result from the merger or consolidation, along with a mitigation plan and future business plans.

[201] Under OJK Regulation No. 9/POJK.04/2018, there are a number of disclosures required for an MTO. These include:

(a) The acquiring company must submit, to the OJK and to the target company, a covering letter, an announcement on the disclosure information required in the context of an MTO and any supporting documents within two working days after the announcement of the acquisition.
(b) In the context of an MTO the acquiring company must submit any amendment and/or additional information required in the text of the announcement, as well as the supporting documents, within five days after receiving a request to do so from the OJK, if the OJK requires the new controlling company to make any such amendment and/or to provide any such additional information.
(c) In the context of an MTO the acquiring company must announce the required disclosure information in one daily newspaper circulating nationally, or on the stock exchange's website, within two working days after receiving a letter from the OJK requiring the new controlling company to announce such disclosure information.
(d) Following completion of the MTO, the acquiring company must submit a report on the result of the MTO to the OJK within five days after completion of the transaction.

[202] The report to OJK on the result of an MTO must contain at least the following information:

(a) number of shares purchased in the MTO;
(b) implementation period for the MTO;
(c) date of completion of the MTO transaction;
(d) list of shareholders selling their shares;
(e) number of shares purchased in the course of implementation of the MTO;
(f) composition of share ownership of the new controller before and after the MTO.

[203] There are no regulations relating to the withdrawal of an MTO. However, if an MTO is withdrawn, the withdrawing company may be punished by sanctions from the OJK. On the other hand, for a 'voluntary' bid, specific regulations apply to withdrawal under OJK Regulation No. 54/POJK.04/2015. These are:

(a) A 'voluntary' bid may generally not be withdrawn, if an announcement of the bid has been issued. However, this requirement may be waived if the OJK approves.
(b) In cases where a 'voluntary' bid is withdrawn, any offered securities must be returned within twelve days after the withdrawal.

[204] Control of the acquired company will pass to the buyer when a deed of acquisition executed before a notary in the Indonesian language has been notified to the MOLHR. 'Control' is defined under Article 1 point (d) of the Capital Market Law (Law No. 8/1995), as the ability to determine, either directly or indirectly, and by any means, the management and/or the policy of the company. In terms of a public company, Article 1 point (4) of OJK Regulation No. 9/POJK.04/2018, stipulates that the controller of a public company is:

(a) a party owning more than 50% of the issued share capital (de jure control), or
(b) a party which is able, either directly or indirectly, to determine the management and/or the policy of the public company (de facto control).

[205] Based on these doctrines, there are several levels of control, which are:

(a) *GMS and AoA*: In the GMS, the controlling party is able to determine the strategic positions of the management and is also in a position to amend the AoA.
(b) *Shares with Special Rights*: A party owning minority shares in the company may nevertheless have special rights attaching to those shares, such as preferential shares.
(c) *Financial Statements*: Where the financial statements of a subsidiary company are consolidated with those of its parent company (the controller), it is clear that the parent is the controller. According to basic accounting principles, if a company owns 50% of the shares of another company, the financial statements of the subsidiary are automatically consolidated with the financial statements of the parent company.

[206] Following an offer, there are two ways of squeezing out recalcitrant or dissenting minority shareholders. These are:

(1) Freeze out
Freeze out is a method used by majority shareholders to force minority shareholders out of a company, by eliminating their status as minority shareholders. This may be carried out after the acquiring company has secured control of a majority of the shares of the target company. In other countries, a freeze out can be carried out legally by means of particular procedures, such as the 'reverse shares fraction'. This involves increasing the nominal value of the shares through an amendment of the AoA, such that a large number of shares is exchanged for a smaller number or a single share. As a consequence the minority shareholder holds a smaller fraction of shares and may thus be forced to sell them.
(2) Squeeze out
A squeeze out is similar to a freeze out in so far as it involves an element of coercion to remove the minority shareholder from the target company. However, in a freeze out, the coercion is directly applied, whereas in a squeeze out the coercion is indirect. For example, after the acquiring company has secured control of a majority of the shares, it may manipulate the

management of the target company to create unpleasant conditions for the minority shareholders, such that they choose to sell their shares. However, shareholders dissenting from the decision of the GMS for acquisition do have a right to be bought out. They have a right to request the company to purchase their shares at a reasonable price, subject to conditions under circumstances where the acquisition is causing loss to the shareholders (*see* Article 62 of Law No. 40/2007)

[207] Under OJK Regulation No. 9/POJK.04/2018, the penalties for violation of the rules on public takeovers are administrative sanctions issued by OJK, including:

(a) Written warnings
(b) Fines, namely the obligation to pay a specific sum of money
(c) Restriction of business activities
(d) Suspension of business activities
(e) Revocation of business license
(f) Cancellation of approval
(g) Cancellation of Registration.

[208] Compliance with the takeover rules cannot be enforced through the courts. Thus the sanctions referred to above are the only recourse to compel a company to comply with the takeover rules.

2.8 Other Relevant Laws and Due Diligence Issues

2.8.1 Anti-Corruption Laws

[209] In Indonesia the bribery of public officials is regulated under Indonesian Law No. 31 of 1999 regarding Eradication of Criminal Acts of Corruption, as amended by Law No. 20 of 2001 (together, the 'Anti-Corruption Law'). However, the Indonesian legal system does not explicitly regulate bribery in the private sector.

[210] While corporations can be subject to criminal sanctions under a number of laws, (such as the Anti-Corruption Law, Anti-Money Laundering Law, Environmental Law, and Forestry Law), there have been few criminal cases where a corporation has been brought before a judge and sanctioned in corruption cases. This follows the issuance of Supreme Court Regulation No. 13 of 2016 on Case Handling Procedures for Corporate Crimes ('SC Regulation No. 13/2016') by the Corruption Eradication Commission (KPK).

[211] SC Regulation No. 13/2016 goes into further detail on liability in cases of mergers, consolidations, spin-offs, and liquidations, and it also governs the liability of a corporation after a restructuring. Generally speaking, restructuring will not relieve a corporation from its liability; the liability will be borne by the successor or surviving corporation. Furthermore, criminal liability is not only limited to corporations but can also be applied to a group of corporations. If a crime is committed by a corporation with its parent or subsidiary or other related corporations, they can also be held accountable for the crime, depending on their roles in the crime.

[212] Furthermore, anti-corruption laws have not been rigorously enforced in the capital market due to the limited competence of the investigators. Therefore the OJK, acting through OJK Regulations No. 29/POJK.04/2016 on the submission of annual reports of listed and/or public companies, requires corporations to put in place a transparent system, including a whistle-blower system whereby any violations may be reported.

[213] In Indonesia, some companies have adopted Anti-Bribery Management System SNI ISO 37001:2016 ('ISO 37001') as a management system for corporations to combat corruption. In addition, KPK has published a guideline for corporations in Indonesia on the creation and implementation of an internal system for the prevention of corruption. The implementation of the guideline does not cancel out corporations' legal accountability in a corruption crime case. However, judges will take the existence of the guideline into consideration when passing sentence in corruption crime cases involving corporations.

[214] The US Foreign Corrupt Practices Act (FCPA) and the UK Bribery Act also may affect M&A activity in Indonesia, in circumstances where the companies carrying out M&A activities in Indonesia originate from the USA or the UK or have a presence there. In addition, some Indonesian companies, especially the public companies, have adopted the FCPA and/or UK Bribery Act as their internal policy.

2.8.2 Money-Laundering Regulations

[215] The money-laundering regulations consist of:

(a) Law No. 8/2010 on the Criminal Acts of Money Laundering.
(b) Presidential Regulation No. 50/2011 on the Implementation Procedure on the Authority of the Central Reporting and Financial Transaction Analysis.
(c) OJK Regulation No. 12/POJK.01/2017 on the Implementation of a Program of Anti-Money Laundering and Prevention of Terrorism Funding in the Financial Service Sector, as amended by OJK Regulation No. 23/POJK.01/2019.

[216] Under this last regulation, the principle of 'know your customer' is the pre-emptive action used to counter money-laundering crime. The implementation of this principle starts with the mechanism of receiving and identifying any customer intending to conduct investment in the capital market. Under this mechanism, a financial services provider must request information on the background and identity of the prospective customer, the objective and purpose of opening the account, and any other information enabling a tighter profile of the prospective customer.

2.8.3 Environmental Laws

[217] Environmental issues have an impact on Indonesian business acquisitions, particularly if the target company is a manufacturing company and/or needs an environmental license of some sort. Therefore, the prospective purchaser will need to consider environmental factors, including compliance with any environmental impact requirement.

[218] There are some significant environmental and product safety laws which need to be considered, including:

(a) Law No. 32 of 2009 on Environmental Protection and Management as last amended by Law No.11 of 2020 on Job Creation.
(b) Law No. 41 of 1999 on Forestry as last amended by Law No.11/2020 on Job Creation.
(c) Government Regulation No. 22/2021 on Implementation of Environmental Protection and Management.

[219] The regulatory environment in terms of foreign investment has been consistently eased, by the enactment of the Job Creation Law, to make it more investor-friendly by cutting bureaucracy wherever possible. For example:

- For business activities that require an environmental impact analysis (AMDAL), the Job Creation Law which amends Law No. 32/2009 (laying out the criteria that businesses must follow to request an AMDAL prior to operation) is now applicable only to businesses that 'have important effects on the environment, social, economic and culture'. Thus only material projects involving an 'important effect' will require an AMDAL. The requirement to obtain an environmental permit is removed as this will now be integrated into the Business Identification Number. Consequently, companies are now only required to obtain an AMDAL approval or to provide a statement letter undertaking to comply with environmental management efforts and environmental monitoring efforts (UKL-UPL) standards, before they are able to obtain a business license.
- The grant of Borrow-to-Use Permits which encompass any significant impacts, extensive coverage and strategic value, no longer require approval by the House of Representatives and are simply issued by the central government, i.e., by the Minister of Environment and Forestry, etc.

2.8.4 Product Safety Laws

[220] The main laws and regulations for product safety are:

(a) Law No. 8 of 1999 on Consumer Protection;
(b) Minister of Trade Regulations on licenses for the distribution of goods;
(c) The Head of Drug and Food Control Board Regulations, which supervise the standard of drugs, foods and beverages distributed in Indonesia;

(d) OJK Regulations on Consumer Protection in the Financial Sector;
(e) Decree of the Minister of Industry and Decree of the Minister of Trade on Indonesian National Standards. These impose mandatory SNI on 544 products, consisting of 521 products of textile and textile product (TPT), 21 products of children toys, and 2 electronic products.

2.8.5 IPR Laws

[221] Since Indonesia became a member of the World Trade Organization by ratifying the GATT (*General Agreement on Tariffs and Trade*), Indonesian regulation on IPR has been enhanced. Consequently much legislation involving IPR has been enacted by the Indonesian Government. The legal protection for IPR under the law consists of several elements, which are:

(a) Subject of protection: The person protected is the owner or holder of the rights.
(b) Object of protection: The objects concerned are all types of IPR regulated under the laws, including copyrights, trademarks, trade secrets, patents, etc.
(c) Registration of the protection: The IPR which are protected are only those that are registered and evidenced by a certificate of registration, except where the laws regulate otherwise (e.g., registration is not a requirement for obtaining copyright protection and related rights under Law No. 28/2014 on copyright.
(d) Period of protection: The law determines for how long the relevant IPR is protected. Thus a trademark is protected for a period of ten years (renewable); a patent is protected for a period of twenty years which may also be extended, and so on.
(e) Legal action of protection: If there is any violation of the IPR, the offender can be punished, both through civil and criminal action.

[222] Thus the registration, protection and enforcement of IPR have been accommodated by the establishment of appropriate legislation on IPR. In the context of a Legal Due Diligence process, any relevant IPR may be audited by obtaining evidence/proof of the relevant certificates and carrying out checks through the appropriate registration office.

2.8.6 Agents and/or Distributors

[223] There is no mandatory compensation on termination of distributor agreements in Indonesia provided the termination complies with the reasons set out under Article 22 of the Minister of Trade Regulation No. 11/M-DAG/PER/3/2006. These are:

(a) Termination based on the mutual consent of both parties.
(b) Unilateral termination, if:
    (i) the company is liquidated;

(ii) the company discontinues the relevant business activities;
(iii) the rights of the distributor/agent are transferred to another party;
(iv) the company is bankrupt;
(v) the agreement is not extended.

[224] In addition, in the case of unilateral termination by the principal, where the principal intends to appoint a new distributor/agent before the registration letter (STP) of the previous one has expired, there should be a clean break between the principal and the former agent/distributor (in the form of a written mutual consent stating that the commitment between the parties is at an end).

2.8.7 Valuation of Intangible Assets

[225] Intangible assets like brands, goodwill and IPR are recognized if they are already in the development phase (and no longer in the research phase) and are thus able to be sold, transferred, or licensed to a third party. If an intangible asset is acquired in the context of a business combination, it will invariably be recognized whether or not it has hitherto been recognized in the acquired company's financial statements.

[226] Issues which may arise on the valuation of intangible IPR assets are the expiry date of the certificate of rights, and whether the relevant rights have been registered in the names of others; and as regards trademarks if the license holders in respect of the trademark are not well recorded. Valuation issues frequently arise where there is a dispute between parties claiming to be exclusively entitled to the IPR in question.

[227] Furthermore, Indonesian tax and/or financial auditors frequently face difficulties during the audit of transfer pricing cases related to intangible property, including a lack of transparency in the company's bookkeeping; limited cooperation in providing data and documents; transfer pricing regulations and problems related to organization and human resources.

2.8.8 'Change of Control' Clauses

[228] It is important during the acquisition process to be aware of clauses dealing with 'change of control' in agreements binding on the target company, as these may affect the obligations and liabilities owed by the target company. Specifically, in the context of bank loan arrangements, such clauses are often included in order to provide legal certainty for the repayment to the bank. Such clauses are governed by Article 1338 of the Indonesian Civil Code which sets out the principle of freedom of contract.

2.9 The Due Diligence Process

2.9.1 The Concept of a Full Due Diligence Investigation Involving Commercial, Financial, Tax, Property, Environmental and Other Issues

[229] As part of the acquisition process the acquiring company and the acquired company will typically agree on arrangements for due diligence in a Memorandum of Understanding between the parties and will also enter into an agreement protecting the confidentiality of the information obtained from the due diligence exercise. However there may often be occasions in which the acquiring and/or the acquired company will request only a limited scope of due diligence. Instead of relying on a seller's due diligence report generated by the target company, the acquiring company will typically conduct their own due diligence.

2.9.2 Investigation or Obtaining Certificates of Title in Relation to Property Due Diligence

[230] Due diligence in connection with property will normally oblige the target company to provide the required documents evidencing ownership of property, and arrangements for these to be checked with the National Land Agency to verify the validity of the relevant certificates. The National Land Agency will issue an Information Letter of Land Registration (SKPT) to explain the historical status of the land designated for investigation based on physical and juridical data. This will include information as to the registered name of the landowner, the physical area of the land, title to the land and any security over the land.

2.9.3 Environmental Audits

[231] Environmental due diligence audits help the acquiring company to identify environmental liabilities prior to purchasing a new property – an important issue in determining its true value. An environmental due diligence assessment will provide an understanding of any contamination issues relating to the site and any potential for legal civil damages that could eventuate.

[232] Furthermore, according to Law No. 32 of 2009 on Environmental Protection and Management as last amended by Law No.11 of 2020 on Job Creation, environmental audit is an evaluation carried out to assess compliance of those in charge of a business and/or activity with legal requirements and policies stipulated by the government. Therefore, it is usual to carry out environmental audits, particularly on businesses and/or activities carrying a high risk to the environment, such as petrochemicals, oil and gas refineries, and nuclear power plants.

2.9.4 Data Rooms

[233] Commonly, the due diligence exercise will make use of 'data rooms' of the target company (whether actual or virtual) in which the required documents will be made available and accessed. However, if the target company does not make available a virtual data room, it should prepare copies of the physical documents together with a due diligence checklist for the legal and/or financial advisors.

2.9.5 Legislative Issues Versus 'Due Diligence' Investigation

[234] Legislative issues that may prove critical to the process of due diligence include any modifications or amendments of laws and regulations affecting the business activities of a company. This may complicate the process of due diligence if the company has failed to adjust to the changes required by applicable laws and regulations. By way of example there may have been revisions to the Negative Investment List which is now called Positive Investment List. Particular issues arise in this context where provisions of the Positive Investment List vary with the different locations where the company performs its business activities. Thus if the Positive Investment List is amended while the company is in the process of due diligence, this may be a serious complicating factor and may extend the time required for due diligence.

2.9.6 Case Study in the Context of Due Diligence and Planning

[235] A further problem which can arise in the context of due diligence and planning is a miscalculation of the financial statements of the target company. Unbooked losses may materialize, for example, where there is an excess of receivables that will be claimed by a third party. An example of such due diligence problems arose in the ABNR law firm v. Sumatra LLC case. The alleged due diligence issues which arose in that case were:

(a) Sumatra LLC had provided a loan in the amount of USD2m to BKPL to purchase trucks, which were guaranteed by a fiduciary security interest in the event of BKPL's failure to repay the loan. The fiduciary guarantee over the twelve trucks was subject to review, but in fact when BKPL defaulted it emerged that the trucks had previously been burdened with a fiduciary security interest to other parties.
(b) Second, and apart from the duplication of the fiduciary security interest, it transpired on a review of the bank guarantee held by BKPL that the bank guarantee used by BKPL was allegedly false.

2.9.7 The Relationship Between the Formal Due Diligence Process and the Imposition of Contractual Representations, Warranties and Indemnities

[236] There is no obligation under Indonesian laws or regulations to carry out due diligence. Nevertheless, in practice, acquisition processes invariably involve a due diligence exercise, because it provides certainty and confirmation to back up the agreed clauses of representations, warranties, and indemnities. The extent to which such clauses are affected by actual knowledge obtained by the purchaser in the course of due diligence, or by the opportunities afforded to the purchaser to investigate and/or verify relevant issues in the course of due diligence will be a matter for negotiation between the parties.

2.10 Role of the Courts

2.10.1 The Role of the Courts

[237] The role of the courts is to examine, decide, and settle cases. Indonesian law includes several options for the resolution of commercial disputes, including, among others, through court litigation. Since commercial disputes are private in nature they generally fall within the jurisdiction of the general court system. However specific commercial courts are also designated to handle specific cases such as IPR, bankruptcy and suspension of debt payments. There is also an Industrial Relations Court, a Tax Court, and a Shipping Court. In addition to the special courts above, there are also quasi-judicial institutions, namely:

(1) The Consumer Dispute Resolution Agency;
(2) The Business Competition Supervisory Commission; and
(3) The Indonesian Broadcasting Commission.

2.10.2 Other Relevant Dispute Resolution Mechanisms in Indonesia

[238] Apart from the court, there are a number of other alternative dispute resolution mechanisms. These include:

(a) Negotiation: In this mechanism, the parties may meet directly in order to jointly discuss the dispute in a cooperative and open manner.
(b) Mediation: Mediation involves voluntary dispute settlement, with the intervention/assistance of an impartial third party, and decision-making by the parties based on consensus and active participation. In the mediation process, there is no element of coercion between the parties and the mediator, because both parties voluntarily request the mediator to assist the settlement of the conflict. Thus the mediator should be impartial and should actively participate in the settlement process.
(c) Conciliation: Conciliation has similarities with mediation. Both mechanisms involve a third party to settle the dispute. However, for conciliation, the conciliator acts not only as a facilitator to arrange and hold the meeting between the parties to resolve their own dispute, but also gives his/her opinions on the dispute, explaining the strengths and weaknesses from parties in order to create the settlement for the parties.

(d) Arbitration: Arbitration is conducted based on a contract between the parties. In arbitration, the power to settle the dispute is vested in the discretion of the arbitrator(s). By contrast with court resolution, which is open to the public, arbitration is not. Arbitration is conducted by means of amicable resolution, with each party generally choosing their own arbitrator to regulate and decide on the dispute.

2.10.3 The Judiciary

[239] The judiciary is independent and has the power to organize the judicature to enforce law and justice. However there are several factors that may sway the decision of the judges. Foremost of these is the origin of the parties. If the dispute is between a domestic resident (or domestic company) and foreigners, the judges have a tendency to support the domestic residents or company over the foreigners, particularly at first and second Instance.

[240] With regard to the competence of the Judiciary, there is absolute competence and relative competence. Absolute competence is vested in four categories of courts (General Court, State Administrative Court, Religion Court, Military Court), as well as the Special Court (Arbitration, Commercial Court, others). Within these categories the jurisdiction of a court cannot be violated by the jurisdiction of a court in any other category. On the other hand, relative competence is assigned to the jurisdiction of courts within the same category.

2.10.4 The Time Generally Taken to Get a Case Heard

[241] The Indonesian judicial system has three main principles, which are simple, fast, and cheap. However, in practice, the implementation of the judicial system is neither simple nor fast nor cheap because, in practice, cases at the appellate levels are backlogged. As a result, this situation may affect the amount it may cost the company to pay its lawyers. In addition, the prevalence of corruption in the judicial system causes the mechanism itself not to work effectively.

[242] If a commercial dispute is pursued through the courts, The Supreme Court has issued circulars and decrees regarding the time frames for handling cases in court, as follows:

(a) District court: five months.
(b) High Court: three months.
(c) Supreme Court: 250 days.

[243] In practice the process may take more time than this, although since 2018 the trend has been for courts to resolve cases faster. This improvement is partly due to the introduction of E-Court. Also, disputes over small claims having a value below IDR500 m are now subject to a small claims settlement procedure, involving simplified evidence and process, and this new procedure is expected to cut the time involved by comparison with existing procedures.

2.10.5 The Enforceability of Key Contractual Provisions

Restrictive Covenants

[244] In relation to restrictive covenants, i.e., clauses aimed at preventing the vendor(s) competing with the business sold, Indonesian law is silent as to the enforceability of such clauses. However, Indonesian law recognizes the principle of freedom of contract, and employers will invariably seek to impose restrictive covenants in their employment agreements and/ or in their collective labour agreements. However they are generally difficult to enforce in practice.

Confidentiality

[245] In relation to confidentiality constraints (including *inter alia* to ensure data privacy and the protection of IPR, including trade secrets), Indonesian law offers statutory protection for the protection of such information provided it meets the statutory definitions within the regulations. Remedies for the theft/misuse of confidential information would include a civil claim for damages or a criminal penalty involving imprisonment or a fine.

Protection of Minority Shareholder Rights

[246] Indonesian law includes a number of regulations designed to protect minority shareholders' rights, whether in a private or public company. For a publicly listed company, any shareholder can in principle claim compensation if he/she suffers damage arising from a business combination.

Warranty or Indemnity Claims

[247] Indonesian law has facilitated the enforcement of warranty or indemnity claims, by requiring sellers to provide accurate information on the characteristics of goods, to provide compensation against warranties and indemnities, and/or to reimburse losses arising from the use of goods and/or services, as regulated under Law No. 8 of 1999 on Consumer Protection.

[248] In addition, there is a Consumer Dispute Settlement Board that can be used to resolve product liability claims in Indonesia, and consumers can also bring class-action claims before the district courts.

3 MERGER CONTROLS & ANTITRUST/ COMPETITION ISSUES

3.1 Relevant Legislation and Competent Authorities

[249] In 2000, the law on anti-monopolistic activities and unfair competition became effective. It is in essence Indonesia's Antitrust Law. The Antitrust Law provides that certain mergers and acquisitions must be approved in advance by the Commission (the supervising body entrusted by the law to deal with failures of compliance and dispute resolution). The criteria for determining which mergers fall under the potential authority of the Business Competition Supervisory Commission (the '**Commission**'/**KPPU**) is provided in Government Regulation No. 57 of 2010 on Merger or Consolidation of Business Entities and Acquisition of Company Shares that could result in Monopolistic Practices and/or Unfair Business Competition.

[250] Merger control and antitrust/competition issues in Indonesia are supervised by the Business Competition Supervisory Commission (*Komisi Pengawas Persaingan Usaha* (KPPU)). One indication of the Commission's authority with regard to mergers is Article 35 on the Duties of the Commission. The duties of the Commission are to conduct evaluations as to whether there is any abuse of dominant position that could result in the occurrence of monopolistic practices and/or unfair business competition as referred to in Articles 25–28. Article 28 deals with proposed mergers and acquisitions and does not deal with concluded mergers to be reported under Article 29. The authorities of the Commission include investigation, summoning, and imposing administrative sanctions in the form of cancellation of mergers and acquisitions of shares as referred to in Article 28.

[251] Of particular note in the Indonesian Antitrust Law are its criminal sanctions. Violations of the provisions of Article 28 are subject to a criminal fine (of at least IDR25bn and not more than IDR100bn) or imprisonment in lieu of a fine for a maximum of six months. Additional criminal penalties can take the form of revocation of a business permit, a prohibition on holding a position as director for at least two years up to a maximum of five years, or the cessation of certain activities that have caused losses to third parties.

[252] In accordance with Article 29 of Law No. 5/1999 and Article 5 (1) of Government Regulation No. 57 of 2010 regarding Merger or Consolidation of Business Entities and the Acquisition of Shares That Can Cause Monopolistic Practices and Unfair Business Competition ('GR No. 57/2010'), the method of evaluation is an evaluation after the merger or consolidation has occurred (post-notification). This means that after the business actors conduct a merger, consolidation or acquisition of shares, the surviving company must notify the KPPU. Such notification must be submitted by completing a form contained in KPPU Regulation No. 3 of 2019 on the Assessments of Merger or Consolidation of Business Entities, or Acquisition of Company's Shares which may Result in Monopolistic Practices and/or Unfair Business Competition ('**KPPU Regulation No. 3/2019**'). Pursuant to Article 29 of Law

No. 5/1999, Article 5 of GR No. 57/2010, and Article 7 of KPPU Regulation No. 3/2019, notification of the relevant merger or consolidation has to be made to the KPPU no later than thirty working days from the date on which such merger, consolidation or acquisition became legally effective. Violations of the provisions of Article 29 of Law No. 5/1999 are subject to an administrative fine of IDR1bn for each day of delay, up to a total of not more than IDR25bn.

[253] Nevertheless, Article 10 of GR No. 57/2010 also provides a right for the business actor to consult the KPPU voluntarily, either in written or verbal form, prior to implementing the merger, consolidation or acquisition. However, Article 20 of KPPU Regulation No. 3/2019 limits the business actor to a written consultation prior to implementation.

[254] As such, based on Article 29 of Law No. 5/1999, and Articles 5 and 10 of GR No. 57/2010, there are two types of evaluation of merger, consolidation, and acquisition that are performed by the KPPU: (a) Post-evaluation ('Notification'), which is mandatory; and (b) Pre-evaluation ('Consultation'), which is voluntary. The evaluation can be conducted personally/proactively by the business actors with the relevant authorities. However, experience in such matters is typically required, either internally or through outside advisors.

3.2 Scope of the Controls

[255] Indonesia's Antitrust Law was promulgated in 1999 and has been in force since 5 March 2000. Despite its title, which refers to the prohibition of 'monopolistic practices', this law contains provisions against 'engineered' market dominance and the control of activities by so-called business actors (as defined below) who already possess a dominant market position.

[256] A monopolistic practice is the concentration of economic power by one or more business actors, resulting in unhealthy (lack of) business competition and potential harm to the public interest. Unfair business competition is competition between business actors (whether in the undertaking of production activities and/or in the marketing of goods and/or services) which is conducted in a dishonest or illegal fashion or which involves the restructuring of business to reduce competition.

[257] A 'dominant position' is defined as a situation in which a business actor has no significant competitor in the relevant market in relation to the market share controlled by that business actor, or in which a business actor has the highest position among its competitors in the relevant market – whether in relation to financial capacity, access to suppliers or sales, or the ability to influence supply and demand for certain goods or services. Finally, a 'business actor' is defined as any individual or business entity, either incorporated as a legal entity or otherwise, established and domiciled in or conducting activities in the jurisdiction of the Republic of Indonesia, whether individually or jointly based on an agreement, conducting various business activities in the economic sector.

[258] Article 16 of the Antitrust Law precludes business actors from entering into agreements with other parties abroad containing provisions which could result in the occurrence of monopolistic practices and/or unfair business competition. In connection with the definition of a business actor as set out above, this means that at least one party must be Indonesian, while the other is foreign. The application of Indonesian Antitrust Law is therefore ruled out in relation to agreements where both parties are domiciled abroad but the effects of their agreement are evident in the Indonesian market. Article 16 only covers 'agreements' and arguably does not cover compliance with statutory obligations as a result of an offshore merger or acquisition.

[259] Business actors are prohibited from conducting mergers or consolidations of business entities that could result in the occurrence of monopolistic practices and/ or unfair business competition. A business actor is also prohibited from acquiring shares in other companies if such acquisition may result in the occurrence of monopolistic practices and/or unfair business competition.

[260] Under KPPU Regulation No. 3/2019, it has been determined that the business actors are required to notify the merger, consolidation or acquisition to the KPPU if it meets the relevant value thresholds unless it is a merger, consolidation, or acquisition between affiliated companies.

[261] The relevant Value Thresholds are as follows:

(1) The asset value of the business entity resulting from the merger, consolidation or acquisition exceeds IDR2 500 000 000 000.00.
(2) The aggregate revenues of the business entity resulting from the merger, consolidation or acquisition exceed IDR5 000 000 000 000.00.
(3) For the banking sector, where the asset value of the business entity resulting from the merger, consolidation or acquisition exceeds IDR20 000 000 000 000.00; or where (if only one of the parties is in the banking sector), the combined asset value within Indonesia exceeds IDR 2.5 trillion; or where the combined sales values of the parties within Indonesia exceed IDR 5 trillion.

Unaffiliated Companies:

Based on the explanation/elucidation of Article 7 of GR No. 57/2010 and Article 6 Paragraph (2) of KPPU Regulation No. 3/2019, 'affiliated' companies are defined as where:

(1) one company, either directly or indirectly, controls or is controlled by the other company;
(2) the companies are controlled, either directly or indirectly, by the same party or parties; or
(3) there is a relationship between the companies and the main shareholder.

[262] Furthermore, KPPU Regulation No. 3/2019 explains that the above definition is also deemed to apply if the affiliation is caused by the ownership of shares constituting less than a 50% majority, but which carry the ability to influence and/or determine the company's policies and/or to influence the management of the company. However, an affiliation of this sort will not be considered as an affiliation as regards the appointment/assignment of directors and/or commissioners who become part of the merger, consolidation or acquisition. Further, the 'main shareholder' as referred to above is the controlling businessman.

[263] An Initial Assessment/test of a Merger, Consolidation, or Acquisition is conducted simply by analysis of market concentration, while some of the following analyses may be used for a Comprehensive Assessment:

(1) market concentration;
(2) barriers to market entry;
(3) potential for anti-competitive behaviour;
(4) efficiency; and/or
(5) bankruptcy.

[264] In addition to the above, pursuant to KPPU Regulation No. 3/2019, KPPU may conduct an assessment in certain matters by using analyses other than those mentioned above, namely:

(1) the policy of strengthening the competitiveness of national industry;
(2) the development of technology and innovation;
(3) the protection of micro, small and medium enterprises;
(4) the impacts on labour; and/or
(5) the implementation of laws and regulations.

3.3 Process/Mechanics

[265] The Law on Prohibition of Monopolistic Practices and Unfair Business Competition provides that any merger or consolidation of business entities or acquisition of shares which results in the value of the assets concerned and/or in the value of sales exceeding certain thresholds must be reported to the Commission no later than thirty days after the date on which the said merger, consolidation or acquisition took place.

Pre-evaluation

[266] Pre-Evaluation is not binding upon the Commission and does not exempt parties from the Post-Evaluation notification requirements. Since the KPPU Regulation No. 3/2019 took effect, there has been no guidance on how the business actor should conduct the Pre-evaluation/consultation. However, business actors could submit their application for Pre-evaluation alongside their merger, consolidation

or acquisition plans by completing the form provided in the Appendix to KPPU Regulation No. 3/2019. Furthermore, the result of the pre-evaluation/consultation process could also be used for the assessment/review process during the post-evaluation/notification, as long there have been no changes of the relevant data for no more than two years.

Post-Evaluation

[267] As mentioned above, within thirty days of the effective date of the relevant transaction, the merger, consolidation or acquisition must be notified to the KPPU. Once the notification form is complete, the Commission has a maximum of sixty working days to clarify and investigate the form providing the information and its supporting documents. The Commission evaluates the merger, consolidation or acquisition transaction based on five aspects, which are as follows: market concentration, entry barriers, anti-competition potential, efficiency, and bankruptcy.

[268] The Commission could issue a Stipulation of Not Mandatory Notification in respect of the relevant transaction if the Commission suggests that: the transaction did not fulfil the relevant tests in relation to assets and/or revenue, and/or that it complied with the definition of an affiliated transaction.

[269] Once the clarification and investigation are complete, the Commission has a further maximum of ninety working days (counting from the date on which the Notification form and its supporting documents were considered complete) to review the transaction. The Commission will issue the Commission's Opinion representing the result of its findings in respect of such transaction. The output of the assessment notification will be that either: (i) there is no potential for monopoly or unfair business competition; or (ii) there is a potential for monopoly and unfair business competition.

[270] To date (that is until the end of December 2020), there have not been any business actors who have conducted a Pre-Notification and/or Post-Notification and who have been considered to have the potential of a monopoly or an unfair business practice.

Sanctions

[271] KPPU is authorized to impose sanctions in the form of administrative actions against businesses who violate the provisions of Article 28 on the merger, consolidation, and acquisition and/or of Article 29 of Law no. 5/1999 on the notification obligation provided for in Article 47 of Law No. 5/1999 as last amended by Law No.11/2020.

(1) Violation of Article 28 of Law No. 5/1999 may be subject to sanctions in the form of:
   (a) the stipulation of cancellation of the said Merger, Consolidation, or Acquisition; and
   (b) the imposition of a minimum fine of IDR1 000 000 000.00.

(2) Violation of Article 29 of Law No. 5/1999 may be subject to sanctions in the form of a penalty incurring a minimum fine of IDR1 000 000 000.00 per day of lateness (maximum IDR25bn) as regulated by Article 6 of GR No. 57/2010. Under KPPU Regulation No. 3/2019, if the parties fail to file a notification, the KPPU does not have to wait until the parties file the notification and will calculate the days of delay up to the date when the KPPU initiates its investigation of such failure.

4 TAXATION ASPECTS

4.1 Nature of the Tax Regime

[272] In recent years the government of Indonesia has made huge strides in resolving taxpayer concerns regarding existing tax legislation and has announced reforms designed to make Indonesia a more appealing destination for investment.

[273] On 26 January 2017, Indonesia signed a multilateral competent authority agreement whereby Indonesia agreed to increase international tax transparency through the automatic exchange of annual Country-by-Country Reports between tax jurisdictions in which multinational groups conduct their operations. Indonesia is also a member of the global forum on transparency and Exchange of Information for Tax Purposes and is the leading international body working on the implementation of global transparency standards around the world.

[274] Indonesia has also completed a tax amnesty programme from 1 June 2016 through to 31 March 2017, which aimed to enable fairer tax reforms through an expanded tax base, to provide a comprehensive and integrated tax database, and to increase voluntary compliance.

[275] In 2019 Indonesia took further steps to simplify the taxation process by introducing an online filing and payment system for major taxes. As a result of these measures, the country ranked 81st out of 190 countries for paying taxes in the World Bank's 2020 Ease of Doing Business index, rising from 112th in 2019.

[276] Thus Indonesia's Tax Regime is heading towards a more certain tax environment, and also enjoys a more transparent tax system. Furthermore, Indonesia is largely a self-assessment tax environment, while enforcement remains a priority for the tax authorities, through the Directorate General of Tax (DGT). In 2020 DGT were aggressively monitoring and enforcing compliance by taxpayers, particularly the making of tax payments.

4.2 Liability to Tax

4.2.1 Tax Subject

[277] Tax subjects are:

(a) individuals and undistributed estates (as opposed to the beneficiaries entitled to inherit such estates);
(b) legal entities; and
(c) Permanent Establishments (the treatment is equivalent to that of a corporate tax subject).

[278] Tax subjects are categorized into two groups; those tax subjects that are resident and those that are foreign tax resident. Law No. 11/2020 on Job Creation makes a significant change in the definition of foreign tax subjects, and introduces the concept of **territorial taxation.** Under the previous law, domestic tax subjects were taxed on their worldwide income.

[279] Parties who are considered as **Tax Residents of Indonesia** are now as set out below:

Law Number 7 of 1983 on Income Tax as amended several times, most recently by Law No. 36 of 2008 on the Fourth Amendment to Law No. 7 of 1983 on Income Tax ('The Previous Law')	*Law No. 7 of 1983 on Income Tax as lastly amended by Law No. 11/2020 on Job Creation ('Income Tax Law')*
(1) **Individuals** who are domiciled in Indonesia, individuals who have resided in Indonesia for more than 183 days within the last 12 months, or individuals who within a taxable year, are resident in Indonesia and intend to become domiciled in Indonesia; (2) entities which are established or domiciled in Indonesia, except for certain units of government entities, which meet the following criteria:	(1) An individual, whether an Indonesian citizen or a foreign citizen[4]who is: (a) domiciled in Indonesia; (b) has resided in Indonesia for more than 183 days within the last 12 months; or (c) within the relevant taxable year is both resident in Indonesia and is intending to domicile in Indonesia;

[4] For a foreign citizen with special skills (to be determined with the minister of finance regulation). The first four-years presence in Indonesia as a domestic tax subject.

Law Number 7 of 1983 on Income Tax as amended several times, most recently by Law No. 36 of 2008 on the Fourth Amendment to Law No. 7 of 1983 on Income Tax ('The Previous Law')	*Law No. 7 of 1983 on Income Tax as lastly amended by Law No. 11/2020 on Job Creation ('Income Tax Law')*
(a) the establishment must be based on laws and regulations; (b) its financing is sourced from the State Budget or a Regional Budget; (c) its revenues are included in the budget of the central government or of a regional government; and (d) its bookkeeping is examined by the state supervision apparatus; and (3) undistributed estates as a unit as opposed to the individuals who are entitled to inherit them.	(2) an entity established or domiciled in Indonesia, except for certain units of government agencies, that meet the following criteria: (a) the establishment is based on the provisions of laws and regulations; (b) the financing is sourced from the State Revenue and Expenditure Budget or the Regional Revenue and Expenditure Budget; (c) the revenues are included in the budget of the central government or regional government; and (d) the bookkeeping is examined by the state functional supervisory apparatus; and (3) an undistributed inheritance as a unity as opposed to the beneficiaries entitled to inherit them.

[280] Parties who are considered as **foreign tax residents** are:

The Previous Law	*Income Tax Law*
(1) Individuals who are not domiciled in Indonesia, individuals who have been resident in Indonesia for less than 183 days within the last 12 months, and entities which are not established and domiciled in Indonesia, which conduct their business or activities in the form of a permanent establishment in Indonesia; and (2) individuals who are not domiciled in Indonesia, individuals who have been resident in Indonesia for less than 183 days within the last 12 months, and entities which are not established and domiciled in Indonesia, which may receive or earn income from Indonesia other than from the conduct of business or the carrying on of activities in the form of permanent establishments in Indonesia.	(1) Individuals who are not domiciled in Indonesia; (2) **foreign citizens** who have been resident in Indonesia for less than 183 days within the last 12 months; (3) **Indonesian citizens who have been resident outside Indonesia for more than 183 days within the last 12 months and who meet the following requirements:** **(a) place of residence;** **(b) centre of main activity;** **(c) place of habitual activities;** **(d) status of the tax resident; and/or** **(e) other specific requirements** which will be further regulated by the Minister of Finance; and (4) entities not established and not domiciled in Indonesia which run a business or carry out activities through a permanent establishment in Indonesia or who may receive or earn income from Indonesia otherwise than from running a business or carrying out activities through a permanent establishment in Indonesia.

4.2.2 Permanent Establishments

[281] A foreign tax resident company carrying out business activities through a Permanent Establishment (PE) in Indonesia may be treated as having a taxable presence in Indonesia and will have the same tax obligations as a corporate tax subject. A permanent establishment is considered a foreign tax resident, which can be in the form of:

(a) a place of management;
(b) a branch of the company;
(c) a representative office;
(d) an office building;
(e) a factory;
(f) a workshop;
(g) a warehouse;
(h) a room for promotion and selling;
(i) mining and extraction of natural resources
(j) a mining working area for oil and natural gas;
(k) a fishery, animal husbandry, agriculture, plantation, or forestry location;
(l) a project of construction, installation, or assembly;
(m) the furnishing of services in whatever form by employees or other people, insofar as conducted for no more than 60 days within a 12-month period;
(n) a person or corporation acting as a dependent agent;
(o) an agent or employee of an insurance company that is not established and domiciled in Indonesia that receives insurance premiums or insures risk in Indonesia; and
(p) the computers, electronic agents, or automated equipment owned, leased, or used by an electronic transactions provider to conduct business via the Internet.

[282] However, activities which are merely preparatory or which are auxiliary in nature to the principal activity are exempted from the definition of a PE.

[283] A PE must obtain a Taxpayer Identification Number (*Nomor Pokok Wajib Pajak* or an NPWP) by no later than one month after the commencement of the PE's business or activity in Indonesia. If a PE does not do so, the relevant Tax Office has a discretion simply to allocate/issue an NPWP to the PE. Once a PE has an NPWP, the PE is required to submit monthly and annual tax returns to the DGT. Indonesian permanent establishments of foreign companies have to settle their tax liabilities either by direct payments, third party withholdings, or a combination of both.

[284] By Article 25 of the Income Tax Law, the monthly tax instalments constitute the first part of tax payments to be made by tax residents of Indonesia and Indonesian PEs as a prepayment of their current year's corporate income tax (CIT) liability. A monthly tax instalment is generally calculated using the most recent corporate tax return. Special instalment calculations apply for new taxpayers, finance lease companies, banks, state-owned companies, listed companies and other taxpayers with periodical reporting requirements.

[285] By Article 23 of the Income Tax Law, tax withheld by third parties on certain income, or tax paid in advance on certain transactions (e.g., Article 22 regarding income tax on imports) also constitute prepayments for the current year's CIT liability of the income recipient or of the party conducting the import.

[286] By Articles 22, 23, and 25 of the Income Tax Law, if the total amounts of tax paid in advance through the year, and Article 24 income tax for the tax paid abroad are less than the total CIT due, the company concerned has to settle the shortfall before filing its corporate income tax return (CITR). Such payment is referred to as Article 29 income tax.

[287] Certain types of income earned by Tax Residents of Indonesia or Indonesian PEs are subject to final income tax. In this respect, the tax withheld by third parties (referred to in Article 4(2) of the Income Tax Law) constitutes the final settlement of the income tax for that particular income. In addition, for foreign companies without PEs in Indonesia, the tax withheld from their Indonesia-source income by the Indonesian party paying the income (Article 26 of the Income Tax Law) constitutes a final settlement of their income tax due. The general Article 26 income tax rate on payments to foreign tax residents remains at 20%. However, under Law No.11/2020 on Job Creation, the applicable tax rate on interest can be lowered by Government Regulation.

4.2.3 The Main Taxes That Potentially Apply to a Business Vehicle Taxable in Indonesia

Corporate Income Tax

[288] Corporate income tax is collected in respect of various types of transaction, including among others the Importation of goods, the sale of goods to the government, the sale or purchase of certain products, the sale or purchase of very luxurious goods, and the payment for certain services.

[289] Law No. 2 of 2020 on The Regulation of the Government in Lieu of Law No. 1 of 2020 on State Finances and the Stability of the Financial System Policies for the Mitigation of Coronavirus Disease 2019 (COVID-19) Pandemic and/or to Deal with Threats that are Potentially Harmful to the National Economy and/or to the Stability of the Financial System ('**Law No.2/2020**') stipulates a lower corporate income tax rate for corporate taxpayers.

Corporate Income Tax	*Tax Rate*
Normal Rate	– 25% applies to net taxable income up to the fiscal year 2019. – 22% applies to net taxable income for the fiscal year 2020–2021. – 20% applies to net taxable income for the fiscal year 2022 onwards.
A public company with >40% of its shares traded on the IDX	– 20% for the fiscal year up to 2019. – 19% for the fiscal year 2020–2021. – 17% for the fiscal year 2022 onwards.

Corporate Income Tax	*Tax Rate*
Companies with a gross turnover below IDR 50bn	12.5% of turnover.
Companies with a gross turnover below IDR 4.8bn	0.5% of turnover.

Taxes on Capital Gains

[290] Capital gains are treated in the same way as ordinary income and are taxed at the standard corporate income tax rate. Please note that the same tax rate applies to corporations as well as individuals, as follows:

- Capital gains derived from the sale of Indonesian assets held by foreigners are taxable at a rate of 5% of the gross proceeds. Non-resident taxpayers may be protected from tax by the provision of any applicable tax treaties.
- The sale of shares listed on the Indonesian Stock Exchange is subject to a final tax at a rate of 0.1% of the gross proceeds, plus an additional 0.5% for founder shares on the share value at the time of the IPO. Certain types of venture capital companies are not required to pay tax on capital gains in certain circumstances.
- The sale of domestic real estate is subject to 2.5% final income tax on the sale price. The purchase of domestic real estate is subject to a 5% tax on the transfer of title.
- Other capital gains derived by residents are included in taxable income and are subject to tax at the normal progressive income tax rates. Other capital gains derived by non-residents are subject to tax at a rate of 20% on an amount of deemed income.

Value Added Tax (VAT)

[291] The VAT rate generally is 10%. This may be increased to 15% or decreased to 5% according to government regulation. Certain goods and services are exempt. Exports of taxable goods, intangibles, and certain taxable services are zero-rated, such as for export of taxable goods.

[292] Law No. 2/2020 introduces new tax treatments for the digital economy business. In general, transactions conducted through an electronic system will be subject to VAT and Income Tax, which will be imposed on foreign companies or individuals.

[293] Furthermore, under Law No. 11/2020 on Job Creation, the transfer of VATable goods in the context of mergers, consolidations, expansions and acquisitions, and capital deposits in exchange for shares are not considered as a VATable delivery, provided that the transferor and the transferee are both VATable Entrepreneurs (*Pengusaha Kena Pajak* (PKP)). In cases where one of those parties is not a PKP the system for implementation is as follows:

- If the transferor is a non-PKP, the transfer is still included in the definition of delivery of VATable goods and hence, VAT is payable but not collected because the transferor is not a PKP.
- If the transferor is a PKP and the transferee is a non-PKP, the transfer is included in the definition of delivery of VATable goods and hence, VAT is payable and normal VAT treatment is applied.

Stamp Duties

[294] A new Stamp Duty Law No. 10 of 2020 has been issued, revoking Law No. 13 of 1985, and took effect from 1 January 2021. Stamp duty applies on the following documents:

(a) documents referable to events of a civil nature; and
(b) documents to be used as evidence in Court.
(c) What is meant by 'documents of a civil nature', includes:
(d) agreements, certificates, statement letters, or similar documents along with copies thereof;
(e) notarial deeds and engrossments, including copies and excerpts thereof;
(f) deeds made by the Land Officer along with copies thereof;
(g) securities in any form and name;
(h) securities transaction documents, including documents for futures contract transactions in any name or form;
(i) auction documents in the form of excerpts, minutes and copies;
(j) documents stating a sum of money above IDR5 000 000; and
(k) other documents stipulated by Government Regulation.

[295] According to the new stamp duty law, stamp duty is imposed once for each document with a flat rate of IDR10 000, as opposed to the system under the previous Law where rates ranged from IDR3 000 to IDR6 000, depending on the amount of the transaction and the type of document.

Taxes on Land Transactions

[296] A transfer of land and building rights will typically also give rise to a duty on the Acquisition of Land and Building Rights (*Bea Pengalihan Hak Atas Tanah dan Bangunan*/BPHTB). BPHTB is based on the Tax Object Acquisition Value (*Nilai Perolehan Objek Pajak*/NPOP), which in most cases is the higher of the market (transaction) value or the Sales Value of the Property (*Nilai Jual Objek Pajak*/NJOP) of the land and building rights concerned. The tax due on a particular event is determined by applying the relevant duty rate of 5% to the relevant NJOP, minus an allowable non-taxable threshold. The non-taxable threshold amount varies by region: the minimum is IDR 60m, except in the case of an inheritance, where the threshold starts from Rp. 300m. Furthermore, various exemptions apply, including transfers made in connection with a merger and transfers to relatives.

[297] A transfer of rights to land and building will give rise to income tax on the deemed gain on the transfer/sale and is charged to the transferor (seller). The tax is set at 2.5% of the gross transfer value (tax base). However, for transfers of simple houses and simple apartments conducted by taxpayers engaged in a property development business, the tax rate is 1%. This tax must be paid by the time the rights to land and building are transferred to the transferee.

[298] Transfers include sale-purchase and trade-in transactions, grants, inheritances, contributions to a corporation, rights separations, buyer designation in an auction, the execution of a court decision with full legal force, business mergers, consolidations, expansions, and prize deliveries.

Land and Building Tax

[299] Land and Building Tax (Pajak Bumi dan Bangunan/PBB) is payable annually on land, buildings and permanent structures. The actual rate is dependent on regional government regulation, but subject to a maximum rate of 0.3% of the estimated sales value of the property determined by the relevant authority. Land and buildings tax and regional taxes may be deducted from taxable income.

Property Value (IDR)	*Tax Rate (%)*
Up to 200m	0.01
200 m to 2bn	0.10
2bn to 10bn	0.20
Over 10bn	0.30

Capital Duties

[300] In Indonesia, there is no capital duty. However, various Non-Tax State Revenue Duties and registration fees apply.

Taxes Imposed on Employers

[301] Employers are required to withhold Article 21 or Article 26 Income Tax on a monthly basis from salaries and other compensation payable to their employees subject to progressive tax rates from 5% to 30%. If an employee is a resident taxpayer, the amount of tax withheld will be based on the normal tax rates. If the employee is a foreign tax resident, the withholding tax is 20% of the gross amount (but may be set at a lower rate under a tax treaty).

Taxable Income	*Tax Rate (%)*	*Tax*
Up to IDR 50m	5	2.5m

Taxable Income	*Tax Rate (%)*	*Tax*
Above IDR 50m–IDR 250m	15	30m
Above IDR 250m –IDR 500m	25	62.5m
Above IDR 500m	30	3% of the relevant amount

[302] The national social security schemes are a Manpower Scheme (BPJS *Ketenagakerjaan*) and a Healthcare Scheme (BPJS Kesehatan), with premiums payable as follows:

Social Security Scheme	*Area Covered*	*Based on the Percentage of Regular Salaries/Wages*	
		Borne by Employers	*Borne by Employees*
Manpower Scheme	Working accident protection	0.24 – 1.74%	–
	Death insurance	0.3%	–
	Old age savings	3.7%	2%
	Pension plan[5]	2%	1%
Healthcare Scheme[6]		4%	1%
			1% for any additional family member

[303] These national security schemes are mandatory for Indonesian citizens as well as for expatriates who work in Indonesia for at least six months. Contributions to a pension plan are not mandatory for expatriates. In addition, expatriates need to be able to prove their participation in the social security schemes when renewing their working permit.

[5] The regular salary/wages cap for calculation the pension insurance contribution is IDR 8 512 400 per month (as per March 2019). The amount may be updated from time to time.

[6] The regular salary/wages cap for calculating the healthcare contribution is IDR 8 000 000. The amount may be updated from time to time.

Customs and Excise Duties

[304] Indonesian law allows import duties to range between 0% and 150% of the customs value of the imported goods, the highest rate currently being set at 40%. The customs value is calculated on the CIF (Cost, Insurance and Freight) value. Indonesia has signed a number of free trade agreements, effectively scrapping or significantly lowering import duty rates. Certain exemptions also apply, e.g., to goods in a bonded zone/warehouse, and to goods in an import facility for export purposes. However, for protectionist purposes/strategies, the government still applies high rates to specific goods. There are also anti-dumping import duty rates applicable to certain products from certain countries.

[305] Export duty may be calculated based on a certain percentage of the customs value (ad valorem) or may be specifically based on a duty rate per quantity in a certain currency. The customs value is determined by the Director General of Customs and Excise in accordance with the price benchmark set by the Ministry of Trade. Upon the issuance of Law No. 2/2020, the Minister of Finance will be authorized to amend lists of goods that are exempted from or given a reduction of Import Duty based on their usage purposes as mentioned in Article 25 and Article 26 of Law No. 10 of 1995 on Customs, as amended by Law No. 17 of 2006 in order to alleviate the effects of the COVID-19 pandemic and threats to the national economy. Excise duties are also imposed on certain goods as part of the government's effort to control the distribution of such goods in Indonesia (e.g., alcohol and tobacco products).

4.2.4 Tax Incentives

[306] Tax incentives available in Indonesia include:

- An income tax reduction of 5% may be available for a Public Company that has at least 40% of its total paid-up shares traded on the Indonesian Stock Exchange, provided certain terms and requirements are met.
- For certain investments the Minister of Finance may provide a tax holiday of 100% of corporate income tax due for a period ranging from five to twenty years from the start of commercial production, depending on the investment amount. After the end of the tax holiday, the relevant companies receive a 50% corporate income tax reduction for two years.
- Tax exemptions for certain transactions, e.g., mergers and spin-offs.
- Tax incentives are available to a business vehicle undertaking capital investment in certain approved industry sectors or operating in certain geographical locations if certain conditions are satisfied. Incentives include a reduction in net income up to 30% of the amount invested, prorated at 5% over six years of commercial production, as long as the assets invested are not transferred out within six years.
- Certain other Corporate Tax Benefits and Tax Allowances.

[307] Furthermore, in order to mitigate the economic impact of the outbreak of COVID-19, the Indonesian Government needed a measure providing more favourable tax treatment for certain activities or sectors compared to the tax treatment accorded to other economic activities in general. This is achieved through the following regulatory policies:

- the Minister of Finance Regulation No. 44/PMK.03/2020 on Tax Incentives for Taxpayers Affected by COVID-19, came into force on 27 April 2020 and related to VAT Incentives, Article 25 Income Tax Incentives, Article 22 Import Income tax Incentives, Final Income Tax Incentives, and Article 21 Income Tax Incentives.
- the Minister of Finance Regulation 143/PMK.03/2020 regarding tax facilities for goods and services required in the handling of the COVID-19 pandemic and the extension of income tax facilities based on Government Regulation (GR) No. 29 of 2020 regarding income tax facilities for handling COVID-19, which came into force on October 1 2020.
- the Minister of Finance Regulation No. 153/PMK.010/2020 on the grant of a deduction in gross income for certain research and development (R&D) activities in Indonesia, which came into force on October 9 2020. The Indonesian government has provided incentives to reduce gross income for 11 specified industries including food, pharmaceuticals, cosmetics and medical devices, textiles, leather and shoes, and means of transportation. Taxpayers conducting certain R&D activities in Indonesia can be granted a deduction from gross income of up to 300% of the total cost expended within a certain period.

4.3 Tax Consolidation: Group Relief of Gains and Losses

[308] There is no provision for tax consolidation or group relief under Indonesian law. Each company is treated as a separate person for tax purposes.

4.4 Tax Considerations Arising on M&A Transactions

[309] The basic tax issues which will arise for the principal parties on M&A transactions include, among others:

4.4.1 Corporate Income Tax on Capital Gains

[310] According to Article 4(1)(d) of the Income Tax Law companies, partnerships and other entities are subject to income tax on gains made from the sale or transfer of property. Taxable gains will arise in the following circumstances:

- When a property is transferred to a corporation in exchange for shares or a capital contribution.
- When a property is transferred to shareholders, partners or members.

- On liquidation, merger, consolidation, expansion, spin-off, acquisition, or reorganization by whatever name or form.
- When property is transferred in the form of a grant, aid or donation. However, there is no taxable gain if the property is given to close relatives, religious bodies, educational or other social entities including a foundation, cooperative, or any individual who conducts micro and small businesses as stipulated by the Minister of Finance. This last exception applies only if the parties have no business, employment, ownership or control relationship.
- On the sale or transfer of all or part of mining rights, participation in financing, or capitalization in a mining company.

		Individual Vendor	*Corporate Vendor*
On a Sale of Shares (for cash, shares or other securities)	From the vendor's perspective	Income tax: 5%–30%	Capital Gains: – 25% applies to net taxable income up to the fiscal year 2019. – 22% applies to net taxable income for the fiscal year 2020–2021. – 20% applies to net taxable income for the fiscal year 2022 onwards. The tax rate is 20% for corporates, where at least 40% of their shares are traded on the Indonesian stock exchange.
		Sale of shares on IDX: Domestic: 0.1% final income tax rate on the proceeds. Founder shareholders may choose to pay tax at 0.5% of the market price of their shares upon listing. Foreign: 0.1% of the gross value of the stocks' transaction.	
	From the purchaser's perspective	There is no tax on an entity acquiring shares	

<table>
<tr><td></td><td></td><td>Individual Vendor</td><td>Corporate Vendor</td></tr>
<tr><td rowspan="3">On a Sale of Assets (for cash, shares or other securities)</td><td rowspan="2">From the vendor's perspective</td><td>Land and Building:
2.5 % final income tax</td><td>the transfer of land and/or building rights:
– The general tax rate: 2.5% of the gross amount
– The tax rate for the sale of low-cost houses: 1% of the gross amount
– The government, a state-owned enterprise, or regionally owned enterprises: 0% of the transfer of land and/or building rights</td></tr>
<tr><td></td><td>Capital Gains:
– 25% applies to net taxable income up to the fiscal year 2019.
– 22% applies to net taxable income for the fiscal year 2020–2021.
– 20% applies to net taxable income for the fiscal year 2022 onwards.</td></tr>
<tr><td>From the purchaser's perspective</td><td colspan="2">There is no tax on the acquisition of assets other than land or buildings.
Land and Buildings: 5% transfer of title tax (duty)</td></tr>
</table>

4.4.2 Stamp Duty

[311] The following are the documents relating to M&A transactions which are charged with stamp duty:

(a) agreements, certificates, statement letters, or similar documents along with copies thereof;
(b) notarial deeds;
(c) deeds made by the land officer;
(d) securities in any form and name;
(e) all documents which involve more than IDR5 000 000.

4.4.3 Price Values

[312] In general, a merger, consolidation, expansion or acquisition transaction should be at fair market value. However, according to the Minister of Finance Regulation No. 52/PMK.010/2017 as amended by Minister of Finance Regulation No. 205/PMK.010/2018 on the Use of Book Value on the Transfer of Assets for Business Mergers, Consolidations, Expansions, or Acquisitions, corporate taxpayers are allowed to use book values on the transfer of assets in the context of business mergers, consolidations expansions, or acquisitions upon approval from the DGT, provided they meet the following requirements:

(a) the application must be filed within six months after the effective date of the business transaction by attaching the reason and purpose of such transaction;
(b) the transaction fulfils the business purpose test; and
(c) a tax clearance letter (Surat Keterangan Fiskal) is obtained for each of the relevant domestic corporate taxpayers or PEs.

[313] However, if the taxpayer does not obtain such approval from the DGT then the transfer of assets will be assessed at market value. Business purpose tests are fulfilled if, among other things, the assets that are approved for transfer using book value are not transferred to a third party within two years after the effective date of the business transaction, unless the transfer is carried out to increase the company's efficiency.

[314] In the case of mergers, consolidations, or acquisitions of a business executed in the current tax year, the amount of instalments of income tax under Article 25 payable by the parties who receive the relevant assets, the transfer may not be less than the amount of instalments of income tax under Article 25 from all relevant taxpayers prior to the relevant transaction having taken place. Settlement of income tax for the current tax year through payment, deduction and/or collection of income tax prior to the merger, consolidation, expansion, or acquisition of business from domestic corporate taxpayers and from permanent establishments who transfer property, can be transferred into current year income tax payments by taxpayers who receive such transfers.

4.4.4 Tax Clearance Letters

[315] A tax clearance letter (*Surat Keterangan Fiskal* – SKF) is a letter or certificate issued by the DGT that applies to both individuals and corporations. It provides written confirmation of a taxpayer's compliance, or that the taxpayer has no outstanding income tax to pay, or meets the requirements for obtaining the relevant service, or falls within the framework for implementing certain activities. These clearances include, among others:

- Procurement of goods and/or services.
- Tax imposition of 0.5% on the transfer of real estate to a Special Purpose Company (SPC) or Collective Investment Contract (KIK) under certain schemes.
- Submission of applications for corporate income tax reduction facilities in special economic zones (KEK).
- Submission of Tax Holiday applications or corporate income tax deduction facilities.
- Filing of non-fiscal facilities for industrial companies or industrial estate companies.
- Certain services and/or other activities that require a Fiscal Certificate.
- Use of book value for the transfer of assets in the context of a merger, consolidation, expansion, or acquisition.
- Submission of requests for VAT or luxury goods VAT repayments to SKK Migas by Cooperation Contract Contractors (K3S).
- Non-bank foreign exchange business activities.

[316] According to guideline PER-03/PJ/2019, the tax office must issue the tax clearance letter no later than 15 working days after submission of the request. The tax clearance letter is only valid for one month from the issue date.

4.4.5 Tax Losses

[317] Unused tax losses in a target company are not available for use by a foreign-owned acquirer or by its subsidiaries. However tax losses of a target company (whether of a private or public company) survive changes of ownership, without any particular threshold limitation and remain available for five-year carry-forward against profits. However, in certain circumstances, this may be extended to ten years under special facilities available for certain regions and/or industries. The available tax losses are subject to possible adjustments based on a tax audit process.

However, based on Minister of Finance Regulation No. 52/PMK.010/2017 as amended by Minister of Finance Regulation No. 205/PMK.010/2018, in the context of tax neutral mergers a company receiving assets transferred at book value is not allowed to use the tax loss carry-forward from the transferor company.

[318] Note that changes in shareholders do not affect the validity of carried forward losses. Also that no foreign losses can be included in the tax computation.

4.4.6 Mechanism to Mitigate Transaction Risk

[319] In order to mitigate transaction risks, there are a number of mechanisms used internationally. These include, among others:

- Deferred payments: in Indonesia these are commonly used as one of the tax incentives and credits available for business (e.g., import tax payments will be deferred for six months in 19 manufacturing sectors);
- Retentions: these are not commonly used by way of security in Indonesia, although the Indonesian Civil Code grants rights to certain creditors to retain title to goods;
- Holdbacks: these are fairly common in US deals, but they are more unusual in Indonesian deals.
- 'Earn-outs': these are not commonly used in Indonesia.

[320] In mergers and acquisition transactions in Indonesia, deposits and escrow mechanisms are more commonly used than the risk-mitigating mechanisms referred to above. The deposit and escrow mechanisms essentially serve the purpose of demonstrating the buyer's good faith.

[321] As regards the question of whether or not specific expenditures are deductible as business expenses, several issues need to be considered. Generally, a deduction is allowed for all expenditures incurred to obtain, collect, and maintain taxable business profits. Acquisition costs include (in addition to the value of the shares or assets acquired) any additional costs incurred in relation to the acquisition, such as advisory fees from the corporate finance advisor and/or legal fees. The value of the relevant shares or assets and associated acquisition costs can be recorded as an asset.

4.4.7 Acquisition Expenses

[322] There are no specific tax regulations setting out the appropriate tax treatment for additional costs related to acquisitions of shares or assets. Therefore parties must comply with the treatment required by the prevailing Indonesian Financial Accounting Standard (PSAK), as follows:

- Acquisition of Shares: in the case of a share deal, there are no restrictions on the deductibility of additional costs. The additional costs are treated as expenses of the year in which the shares were acquired (PSAK 22).
- Acquisition of Assets: the additional costs of those assets having a useful life exceeding one year are capitalized and depreciated over the period of useful

life (PSAK 16). The depreciation expenses could be charged as expenses proportionally over 4 years, 8 years, 16 years, or 20 years, using the straight-line or double declining balance methods.

4.5 Structuring the Investment

[323] Indonesia, one of the largest economies in the world, has developed specific regulations and guidance on tax to stimulate investment. There are some appropriate methods of structuring transactions, including tax-efficient financing and pre-sale dividend restructuring, under the regulations referred to below:

4.5.1 Withholding Taxes

[324] In general, the regulations on Withholding Taxes are as follows:

	Tax Resident of Indonesia	*Foreign Tax Resident*
Dividends paid to foreign corporate/group shareholders	15%	20%
Dividends paid to foreign individual shareholders	10 % final If the recipient holds at least 25% of the shares, dividends are exempt from tax	
Dividends received from foreign subsidiaries/ affiliates	15%	5%–30% foreign tax credit claimable
Interest paid to foreign corporate/group shareholders or affiliates	15%	Remains at 20%. However, under the Job Creation Law, the applicable tax rate for interest can be lowered by a Government Regulation
Interest received from foreign corporate/group shareholders or affiliates	5%–30% foreign tax credit claimable	–

	Tax Resident of Indonesia	*Foreign Tax Resident*
Intellectual property (IP) royalties paid to foreign corporate/group shareholders or affiliates	15%	20%
Intellectual property (IP) royalties received from foreign corporate/group shareholders or affiliates	5%–30% foreign tax credit claimable	–
Management or consultancy fees paid to foreign corporate/group shareholders or affiliates	2%	20%
Payments to foreign tax residents in respect of the purchase or renting of immovable property	10%	20%

[325] Law No. 11/2020 on Job Creation makes a significant change to the way dividends (both domestic and foreign) and certain offshore income receipts are taxed in Indonesia. These changes essentially provide a more attractive tax regime, especially for investors willing to reinvest these incomes in Indonesia for a certain period. The following are the types of income which are exempt from tax:

	The Previous Regulation	*Income Tax Law*
Dividends paid to foreign corporate/group shareholders and foreign individual shareholders	Dividends received by: (a) Corporate tax resident of Indonesia owning > 25% are not subject to income tax; (b) – Corporate tax resident of Indonesia owning < 25% are subject to income tax at the normal rate; and (c) Individual tax resident of Indonesia are subject to final income tax of 10%.	Dividends from Indonesia that are received by: (a) Individual tax residents of Indonesia (there is an additional requirement that they must reinvest the dividends in Indonesia within a specific period), and/or (b) Corporate tax residents of Indonesia, are not subject to income tax (they are excluded from the income tax objects).

	The Previous Regulation	*Income Tax Law*
Dividends received from foreign subsidiaries/ affiliates	This type of income is taxable in Indonesia using the foreign tax credit mechanism if such income has already been taxed abroad.	Dividends originating from abroad and after-tax earnings of a PE abroad are not subject to income tax in Indonesia, insofar as they are invested or used to support other business activities in Indonesia within a certain period and are received from: (a) Dividends invested in Indonesia which are not subject to income tax; (b) If the investment is <30% of the after-tax earnings of the foreign corporation, the residual balance of 30% less the actual amount invested in Indonesia will be subject to income tax; (c) The excess of earnings after-tax of the foreign corporation after reduction for the amounts specified in paras a & b above, will not be subject to income tax.

[326] Furthermore, there are regulations related to double tax treaties which are stipulated in Regulation of The Director General of Tax Number PER-25/PJ/2018 on Procedures for The Implementation of Double Taxation Avoidance Agreement ('Director General of Tax Regulation No. PER-25/PJ/2018'). The Director General of Tax Regulation No. PER-25/PJ/2018 states that foreign tax residents receiving and/or acquiring income from Indonesia may take advantage of agreements to obtain avoidance of double tax treatment (Avoidance of Double Taxation Agreement (P3B)) where the income recipients are not Tax Resident in Indonesia, where the income recipients are individual persons or entities Tax Resident in Indonesia and enjoying P3B partner country or partner jurisdiction status, there is no misuse of P3B, and the income recipients are the beneficial owners if so required in P3B. In order to take advantage of the Director General of Tax Regulation No. PER-25/

PJ/2018, the foreign tax resident has to submit a Certificate of Residence to the Tax Service Office whose working area encompasses his place of residence, his place of business, or his place of domicile, by no later than the expiry of the periodic tax return submission deadline. At the moment, 67 tax treaties have been identified to which it is intended to apply the legislation.

4.5.2 Debt Financing

[327] In general, all legitimate business expenses directly or indirectly incurred for the purpose of obtaining, collecting, and maintaining taxable income are deductible from assessable income, subject to the requirement for documentary support. The costs associated with the acquisition, incorporation and expansion of the capital of a company can be claimed in full in the year in which the relevant expenditures were incurred, or can be amortized.

4.5.3 Thin Capitalization

[328] Due to a large number of thin capitalization practices used by companies as a means of evading tax, the government through the Minister of Finance issued the Minister of Finance Regulation No. 169/PMK.010/2015 concerning the Determination of a Company's Debt to Equity Ratio for Income Tax Calculation Purposes. This thin capitalization regulation adopts the arm's length pricing principle. The regulations state that the Debt to Equity Ratio (DER) should be a maximum of 4:1, with effect from Fiscal Year 2016 onwards. This is applicable to all taxpayers, except for certain sectors, such as financial services and infrastructure.

[329] Moreover, The Director General of Taxation has issued Regulation of Director General of Taxation No. 25/PJ/2017 on implementation of the Determination of Amount of a Company's Debt to Equity Ratio for Purpose of Calculating Income Tax and Procedure for Reporting Foreign Private Debt, by applying the 4:1 DER and by including an obligation to report the DER calculation and details of the private overseas loan to the Director General of Taxation as part of the company's income tax return.

4.5.4 Transfer Pricing

[330] In the Context of Article 18 paragraph (3) of the Income Tax Law the DGT is able, after the fact, to reallocate income and debt of taxpayers who/which are in a special relationship. The taxable income can be recalculated using certain price comparison methods for sales between independent parties, including the resale price method, the cost-plus method, as well as other methods. A special relationship is deemed to exist, under Article 18 paragraph (4) of the Income Tax Law, if:

(a) The taxpayer has a participation, whether directly or indirectly, in at least 25% of the capital of another taxpayer; or where there is a relationship between taxpayers through common ownership by a third party of at least a 25% participation in the capital of two or more Taxpayers; or
(b) Where one taxpayer controls the other taxpayer or where two or more taxpayers are under common control, either directly or indirectly; or

(c) Where there is a family relationship (either biologically or by marriage) in vertical and/or horizontal lineage of the first degree.

[331] In 2010 the DGT issued an implementing transfer pricing regulation, DGT Regulation No. PER-43/PJ/2010, on Implementation of the Arm's Length Principle, as amended by DGT Regulation No. PER-32/PJ/2011. The scope of application of the Arm's Length Principle covers:

- International related party transactions conducted by a tax resident of Indonesia taxpayer or by a PE in Indonesia.
- related party transactions between tax residents of Indonesia, if these are carried out for the purpose of enjoying different (reduced) tax rates, such as final and non-final income tax for certain businesses, the imposition of sales tax on luxury goods, or transactions conducted with oil and gas contractors.

[332] In relation to the DGT's authority to conduct investigations, note that DGT Regulation No. PER-32/PJ/2011 deletes the previous authority conferred on the DGT to investigate a company undertaking a related party transaction with a company indicated to have conducted a tax criminal act.

[333] In line with Action 13 (Transfer Pricing Documentation) of the Base Erosion and Profit Shifting (BEPS) project, the Ministry of Finance issued Regulation No. 213/PMK.03/2016, and DGT Regulation No. PER-29/PJ/2017, which provide detailed provisions on Country-by-Country Reporting (CbCR). The transfer pricing documentation consists of a Master File, Local File, and/or CbCR. The taxpayer is required to file such documents with the corporate tax return, and any incorrect or incomplete tax return may result in a penalty.

5 EMPLOYMENT CONSIDERATIONS

5.1 Legislative Framework

[334] Law No. 13 of 2003 Regarding Manpower as last amended by Law No. 11 of 2020 ('Manpower Law') regulates general matters falling within the scope of labour and employment. In addition, the new legislative framework affecting labour and employment in Indonesia include, among others:

- Government Regulation No. 34 of 2021 on the Utilization of Foreign Manpower ('GR No. 34/2021')
- Government Regulation No. 35 of 2021 on Fixed Term Employment, Outsourcing, Working Hours and Rest Times and Termination ('GR No. 35/2021')
- Government Regulation No. 36 of 2021 on Wages ('GR No.36/2021')
- Government Regulation No. 37 of 2021 on the Job Loss Security Program ('GR No. 37/2021'); and
- specific matters such as regional minimum wages or foreign worker usage are regulated under implementing regulations.

5.2 Employment Protection

5.2.1 Employment Protection Legislation in Indonesia

[335] In Indonesia, the principle of employment continuity on the transfer of a business is not provided for by regulation. Workers and/or their employment contracts do not automatically transfer to a purchaser of a business by operation of law. The purchaser is still able to pre-select those workers he wishes to keep and those he wishes to dispense with. Under Article 154A paragraph (1a) of the Manpower Law as amended by the Job Creation Law, workers have a choice if they do not agree to continue their employment. And, vice versa, the purchaser also has the right to reject workers of an acquired company in the event of a change in the status of the company through a merger, consolidation or acquisition.

[336] There is no requirement that workers be entitled to management representation on either the BoD or the BoC. Management representation is regulated by Company Law. However a company's AoA may provide a procedure and requirements relating to management representation.

[337] A company which is about to conduct a merger or acquisition is obliged to announce it in writing in advance to affected workers of the company about to undergo the merger or acquisition. Notification must be made at least thirty days prior to the call/invitation to the GMS, in order to allow workers an opportunity to understand the plan and to raise objections if it is detrimental to their interests. In relation to an asset sale, the announcement to workers is not mandatory, but nevertheless in practice such an announcement is typically made.

[338] Workers' opinions can be expressed and can impact the stakeholders' decision, as if the workers are not satisfied with the planned action, they have the option to resign. Employers who wish to dismiss workers must notify the individual or the worker's union. In cases where the worker has been notified and refuses it, the matter must be resolved by bipartite negotiation between the employer and the worker and/or the worker's union. If the bipartite negotiation fails, the matter will be determined pursuant to mechanisms for the resolution of industrial relations disputes.

[339] Worker's unions have significant power within the company. The worker's union acts as a supervisor to prevent labour rights being breached. The worker's union also can act as a negotiator in cases where there is a dispute between the employer and the worker and can also act as a representative for the worker if the dispute is brought to the industrial relations court. The worker's union also has rights to contribute to the making of company regulations. And the worker's union has the right to organize a labour strike.

[340] Workers are entitled to be informed or consulted in relation to other corporate transactions, including, e.g., mass layoffs. However, the worker's union itself does not exercise any rights but serves as a body to facilitate negotiations and, in some cases, to help settle disputes depending on the terms of the Collective Labor Agreement (CLA) and applicable laws. It is not possible for employers to contract out of or derogate from mandatory employment protections to the detriment of the employee.

5.2.2 The Regulation on Termination of Individual Employment Contracts

[341] In the case of dismissals occurring, workers are entitled to obtain severance pay, service/tenure awards and compensation. Severance pay, service/tenure awards and compensations must be paid in cash. The minimum amounts of severance pay are calculated as follows:

(a) for a working period of less than one year: one month of wages;
(b) for a working period of one year or more, but less than two years: two months of wages;
(c) for a working period of two years or more, but less than three years: three months of wages;
(d) for a working period of three years or more, but less than four years: four months of wages;
(e) for a working period of four years or more, but less than five years: five months of wages;
(f) for a working period of five years or more, but less than six years: six months of wages;
(g) for a working period of six years or more, but less than seven years: seven months of wages;
(h) for a working period of seven years or more, but less than eight years: eight months of wages;
(i) for a working period of eight years or more: nine months of wages.

[342] The minimum amounts of service/tenure awards are as follows:

(a) for a working period of three years or more, but less than six years: two months of wages;
(b) for a working period of six years or more, but less than nine years: three months of wages;
(c) for a working period of nine years or more, but less than twelve years: four months of wages;
(d) for a working period of twelve years or more, but less than fifteen years: five months of wages;
(e) for a working period of fifteen years or more, but less than eighteen years: six months of wages;
(f) for a working period of eighteen years or more, but less than twenty-one years: seven months of wages;
(g) for a working period of twenty-one years or more, but less than twenty-four years: eight months of wages;
(h) for a working period of twenty-four years or more: ten months of wages.

[343] Compensation will also include:

(a) compensation for annual leave not yet taken or expired;
(b) cost or expenses for workers and their families to return to places where they can take up alternative work;
(c) other matters provided for in the collective labour agreement, company policy or work agreement.

[344] Wages as the basis for payment of severance pay, service/tenure awards, and compensation will comprise:

(a) principal wages;
(b) any and all kinds of fixed allowances given to workers and their families.

[345] In the case of workers receiving wages on a daily basis, the monthly wage is equal to the daily wage times 30 (thirty). In the case of workers paid on the basis of per unit results, the wages for one month equate to the average monthly wage received over the last twelve months. If the monthly wage calculated on the basis of per unit results is lower than the regional minimum wage, the severance pay is calculated on the basis of the minimum regional wage of the company's domicile.

[346] The worker also receives an additional six months of wages from Job Loss/Unemployment Security benefit. To be eligible for this benefit, the worker, as a participant in *BPJS Ketenagakerjaan,* has to pay the associated premium. However, according to Article 46C paragraph (2) of the Job Creation Law (social security section), the central government will pay the premium. The participant will also be eligible for job training and job market information.

[347] If the worker is unwilling to accept the termination of his/her employment, the worker in question may bring this matter to a bipartite negotiation. If the negotiation fails, the worker may file a suit with the Industrial Relations Court.

[348] It is not possible for employers to contract out of these entitlements. If termination of employment takes place, the entrepreneur is obliged to pay the dismissed worker severance pay, service/tenure awards, and compensation pay for any rights or entitlements that the dismissed worker has not utilized. If the employer tries to contract out/derogate from these entitlements to the detriment of the worker and has failed to comply with the mandatory requirements, the employee may refer the dispute to the local office of the Ministry of Manpower and Transmigration, and ultimately to the industrial relations court.

[349] The Manpower Law makes no distinction between blue-collar workers and white-collar workers. According to the Manpower Law, a worker is every person who works for a wage or other forms of remuneration. Since the definition of a 'worker' in the Manpower Law does not make any distinction between blue-collar workers and white-collar workers, we can conclude that both of them fall within the same category for the purposes of that law. However, this definition is not applied to the BoD or BoC since they are regulated under the Company Law.

[350] Labour costs in Indonesia are regulated by the relevant governor. The governor may also determine the regency/city minimum wage under certain conditions in accordance with the economic growth or inflation of the said regency/city.

However, the minimum wage of such regency/city must be higher than the provincial minimum wage.

[351] Unions generally have significant power to negotiate and to set the minimum wage. In cases where there is no agreement on the amount of the minimum wage, unions may frequently conduct demonstrations and/or labour strikes.

5.3 Pensions

[352] Pension provision in Indonesia for companies and their workers is governed under Law No. 11 of 1992 on Pension Funds ('Pension Fund Law'), under which a private sector employer is not required to provide a pension plan to a worker. The requirements for a worker in order to be a participant of a pension fund according to the Pension Fund Law are:

(a) Every worker fulfilling the requirements to be a participant has a right to be a participant if they are at least 18 years old or married and have had a period of employment of at least one year. The requirements for becoming a participant are not clearly stated, because in practice the law deals with pension fund policy as stipulated by the founders and as legalized by the Minister of Finance. The provision defining the normal pension age will be stipulated in the Pension Fund Regulation and may not exceed the provision stipulated by the Minister of Manpower Regulation.
(b) There are two types of pension fund fees – namely the employer fee and the participant fee. If the pension fund determines the participant fee, the employer collects the fee from the participant every month. The amount of the participant fee may not exceed the amount stipulated by the Minister of Finance.
(c) If the founders and/or their partnership are unable to fulfil their obligation to pay the pension funds to the participant, then the participation of the participant may be suspended or terminated.
(d) Participants may not use the pension funds as collateral for a loan, and the funds cannot be transferred out or diverted.

[353] Any corporate action such as a merger, acquisition, or consolidation which might impact the re-arrangement of the company management, including employment, does not affect the performance of existing pension funds. This is because pension funds are an independent legal entity established by their founders which consist of:

(a) Individuals or entities which established the Employer Pension Fund.
(b) Banks or insurance companies which establish the Financial Institution Pension Fund.

[354] The founders may be the employer or their partnership that employ the worker. Therefore, so long as the founders still exist in the company after the relevant company actions, pension funds can still conduct their activities according to their pension fund rules/regulations. However, if there is a change of the founders, pursuant to the Pension Funds Law, the administrator must make changes to the relevant pension fund rules, or if the pension fund is dissolved, it may only be conducted following permission from the Minister of Finance.

[355] Under the individual pension fund rules/regulations, all pension contributions together with interest are allocated to the worker when they resign or are dismissed. The worker cannot normally continue his contributions to the financial institution pension fund following his dismissal or resignation.

[356] Besides the pension fund as referred to in Pension Fund Law, a worker can receive pension benefit from *BPJS Ketenagakerjaan,* the social security programme arranged by the government. To be eligible for this benefit, the worker must be a participant and have paid the associated premiums. There are a few types of pension benefit in this type of social security, such as:

(a) pension due to old age, received by a participant who has attained the age of 57 and has been a participant for a minimum of fifteen years, until he/she dies;
(b) disability pension, received by a participant due to disability caused by accident or illness, until he/she dies;
(c) widower pension, received by a widow as the successor of the participant, until the widow dies or marries again;
(d) child pension, received by a child as the dependant and heir of the participant, until the age of 23, or until he/she gets employed or marries; or
(e) parents' pension, received by parents as the dependants of a participant who was still unmarried, until the parents die.

[357] The benefit is provided monthly in the form of cash. The amount of the benefit is calculated based on a percentage of the relevant wage, or a certain amount that was shared between the worker and the employer.

5.4 Non-compete Clauses

[358] Effective steps available to purchasers to ensure the continuation of individual vendors, members of the management team or other key employees include, among others, a custom for the offer letter to be co-signed by the prospective purchaser who will obtain control over the management of the company, confirming or guaranteeing continued employment after closing.

[359] Moreover, the Manpower Law does not explicitly require or regulate non-competition obligations of workers except for the chief representative of the local representative office of an overseas principal. In any case, Indonesian law recognizes the principle of freedom of contract. This principle is codified in Article 1338 of the Indonesian Civil Code (the Civil Code).

[360] As to non-competition during the period of employment, it is important to include a provision in the employment agreement imposing a duty on the employee not to compete or otherwise to act in conflict with the interests of the employer. A similar arrangement may be set out in the so-called Company Rules/Regulations, or in the Collective Labor Agreement (CLA) if there is a union representing a majority of workers. Infringement of that contractual duty would constitute grounds for termination. However, the enforceability of such post-employment limitations is less clear. There is no jurisprudence on the issue and consequently no clear guidelines as to the requirements for such clauses to be enforceable. Depending on the specific circumstances, such requirements may violate Article 27(2) of the Indonesian Constitution, which vaguely guarantees every citizen the right to work and a decent livelihood. We do not routinely include non-compete or non-solicitation clauses in the employment contracts of ordinary employees.

[361] The enforceability (or not) of non-competition and non-solicitation covenants would probably depend on the specific facts and context. Practically speaking, at least for multinationals operating in Indonesia, it is common for the former employer to alert the new employer about the existence of such constraints, as well as about any confidentiality obligations affecting former employees, and to address the concern in an amicable fashion, recognizing that all companies face the same challenge concerning their previous key employees now and again. Injunctive relief is not generally available in the Indonesian courts. In principle, an employer could sue its former employee for breach of contract by filing a civil lawsuit in the district court system – not the labor courts – for direct damages under Articles 1243–1252 of the Civil Code.

5.5 Treatment of Foreign Workers

[362] It is important to be aware that there are specific restrictions affecting foreign workers. Employers are specifically prohibited from recruiting foreign workers for positions listed in the Appendix of Minister of Manpower Decree No. 349 of 2019 on Occupations that are Closed to Foreign Workers, covering:

(a) Personnel Director
(b) Industrial Relations Manager
(c) Human Resources Manager
(d) Personnel Development Supervisor
(e) Personnel Recruitment Supervisor
(f) Personnel Placement Supervisor
(g) Employee Career Development Supervisor
(h) Personnel Declare Administrator

(i) Personnel and Career Specialist
(j) Personnel Specialist
(k) Career Advisor
(l) Job Advisor (*Penasihat Tenaga Kerja*)
(m) Job Advisor and Counselling (*Pembimbing dan Konseling Jabatan*)
(n) Employee Mediator
(o) Job Training Administrator
(p) Job Interviewer
(q) Job Analyst
(r) Occupational Safety Specialist.

[363] Foreign workers are thus precluded from occupying a position in charge of human resources and/or certain associated positions. An individual employer is also prohibited from engaging a foreign worker. In addition, foreign workers may have more than one position in other companies at the same time listed in GR No. 34/2021, including:

(a) Non-shareholder Director or Commissioner; or
(b) Positions in certain sectors including education and vocational training, the digital economy sector, as well as the oil and gas sector for contractors who utilize cooperation contracts.

However, the first employer must give its consent to the second hiring.

[364] Minister of Manpower Regulation No. 10 of 2018 on the Procedures for Recruitment of Foreign Workers ('Foreign Manpower Regulation') regulates foreign workers, who are required to meet the following criteria in order to work in Indonesia. Specifically they must:

(a) possess adequate educational qualifications;
(b) possess certificates of competence or have had at least five years working experience within the relevant business sector;
(c) engage in the transfer of their skills to domestic co-workers;
(d) possess an official taxpayer identification (NPWP) if the foreign worker has worked in Indonesia for more than six months; and
(e) possess a valid Limited-Stay Residency Permit (ITAS).

[365] Every employer employing foreign workers must have a written permit from the Minister of Manpower, namely a Foreign Worker Recruitment Plan (*Rencana Penggunaan Tenaga Kerja Asing – 'RPTKA'*), and from the Immigration Official, namely a Visa Approval Certificate; VITAS; ITAS; Re-entry Permit and Services for the Utilization of SIMKIM. According to Article 15 paragraph (4) of the Foreign Manpower Regulation, where all documents required have been submitted, the RPTKA will follow within 2 (two) working days. The submissions for these documents are free of charge.

[366] According to GR No. 34/2021, the provision requiring an employer who employs foreign workers to have an approved RPTKA does not apply to:

(a) BoD or BoCs with certain shareholding thresholds referred to in relevant laws and regulations;
(b) diplomatic and consular staff at representative offices of foreign countries; or
(c) foreign workers required by employers in certain types of production activities halted by reason of emergencies, or for vocational activities, technology-based start-up companies, business visits, and research activities for a limited period.

[367] During the COVID-19 pandemic, the Ministry of Law and Human Rights issued Minister of Law and Human Rights Regulation No. 26 of 2020 on Visas and Stay Permits in Adapting to the New Normal ('Regulation 26/2020') which governs the criteria and requirements for a foreigner to enter the territory of the Republic of Indonesia. There is no information to indicate whether these requirements will continue to prevail after COVID-19 is over. According to Article 2 paragraph (1) of Regulation 26/2020, a foreigner who holds a valid visa and/or stay permit, as well as an APEC business travel card can enter the territory of the Republic of Indonesia through a specific immigration checkpoint and following a specific health protocol. For the time being the minister will not issue any Visa on Arrival, visa exemptions or free visit visas (*bebas visa kunjungan*) until the COVID-19 pandemic is officially over. The types of visa and/or stay permit that may be given to a foreigner are as follows:

(a) Official Visa (*Visa Dinas*);
(b) Diplomatic Visa;
(c) Visit Visa;
(d) Limited Stay Visa (*Visa Tinggal Terbatas*);
(e) Official Stay Permit (*Izin Tinggal Dinas*);
(f) Diplomatic Stay Permit;
(g) Limited Stay Permit (**ITAS**); and
(h) Permanent Stay Permit (**ITAP**).

[368] A Visit Visa will be given for these reasons:

(a) emergency work;
(b) business discussions;
(c) purchasing items;
(d) compliance with the fit and proper test for prospective foreign workers;
(e) support personnel for medical and food assistance; and
(f) joining transportation located within Indonesia.

[369] A limited Visit Visa can be given for work purposes or for non-work purposes. For work purposes, a Visit Visa covers:

(a) working as an expert;
(b) working on a vessel, rig or any installation operated in Indonesian territorial waters or in an Economic Exclusive Zone;
(c) for the control of product quality;

(d) for Inspecting or auditing at a company branch;
(e) for providing after-sales services;
(f) for carrying out non-permanent work for construction purposes; and
(g) attending a fit and proper test

[370] The Visit Visa or the Limited Stay Visa will be given in the form of an e-Visa. To obtain a Visit Visa and/or a Limited Stay Visa, the employer, acting as a guarantor of the foreign worker, must submit a request, via electronic means, to the Directorate General of Immigration. In the submission, the guarantor must attach the following documents:

(a) a health certificate issued by the authorized agency of the foreigner's country of origin, written in English;
(b) a letter written in English stating that the foreigner is willing to be put into quarantine or health facilities paid for by the foreigner's own money if the PCR test result proves to be positive or if the foreigner shows COVID-19 symptoms;
(c) a letter stating that the foreigner is willing to be observed during quarantine;
(d) health insurance/travel insurance with proof of payment, and/or a letter stating that the foreigner is willing to pay with his/her own money if he/she contracts COVID-19 in Indonesia.

[371] For the applicant for a Visit Visa, the guarantor has to attach a bank statement showing that the foreigner has minimum funds of **USD**10,000 or equivalent from an Indonesian financial agency or bank. A foreigner who has already held a Limited Stay Permit or a Permanent Stay Permit can submit a stay permit extension to the Directorate General of Immigration. The foreigner is also able to convert the Limited Stay Permit into a Permanent Stay Permit.

[372] In Indonesia, the criteria used for tax purposes include tax on income from Indonesia and any income from overseas sources which is related to employment/service/activity in Indonesia. Tax subjects are divided into domestic tax subjects and foreign tax subjects, both being taxed in Indonesia in the following circumstances:

[373] Domestic tax subjects include:

(1) an individual, whether an Indonesian citizen or a **foreign citizen** who:
  (a) resides in Indonesia;
  (b) has been in Indonesia for more than 183 days within 12 months; or
  (c) resides in Indonesia in a tax year and has the intention to reside in Indonesia;
(2) an entity established or domiciled in Indonesia (except for certain units of government agencies) that meet the following criteria:
  (a) the establishment is based on the provisions of laws and regulations;
  (b) the financing is sourced from the State Revenue and Expenditure Budget or the Regional Revenue and Expenditure Budget;

(c) the revenues are included in the budget of the central government or regional government; and
(d) the bookkeeping is examined by the state functional supervisory apparatus; and
(3) an undivided estate (inheritance) as a unity – as opposed to the beneficiaries of that estate.

[374] Foreign tax subjects include:

(a) individuals who are not resident in Indonesia;
(b) foreign citizens who are in Indonesia for no more than 183 days within 12 months;
(c) Indonesian citizens who are outside Indonesia for more than 183 days within 12 months and who meet the relevant requirements in terms of residence; main activity centre; a place to practice habits; tax subject status; and/or other specific requirements; and
(d) entities not established and not domiciled in Indonesia who run a business or carry out activities through a permanent establishment in Indonesia or who may receive or earn income from Indonesia otherwise than from running a business or carrying out activities through a permanent establishment in Indonesia.

[375] Foreign workers who meet the requirements of domestic tax subjects or (as the case may be) foreign tax subjects are required to register for a taxpayer identification number (NPWP). The twelve-month period is based on the immediately preceding twelve months period and is not a calendar year. The 'intention' to live in Indonesia is evidenced by such actions as applying for a work-permit, owning or renting a house for an extended period, and bringing family members to Indonesia. In addition, it should be noted that, according to the law, those who must pay Indonesian income taxes if they have been here for more than 183 days in a calendar year, include those expatriates here on KITAS, KITAP, business visas or social/visit visas.

[376] The employer must also pay USD 100 per position per worker per month for the Compensation Funds for Utilization of Foreign Worker (*Dana Kompensasi Penggunaan Tenaga Kerja Asing* (DKP-TKA)). The employer must also pay for the foreign worker's social security contributions (BPJS) for foreign workers who worked for more than six months since foreign workers are also considered as participants in the BPJS. According to BPJS Law, the employer is obliged to register their workers for social security purposes. However, according to the GR No. 34/2021 for foreign workers who are working for less than six months must be registered in an insurance programme covering at least the risk of occupational accident.

[377] A director of a company in Indonesia has a responsibility to run the company in accordance with the company's mission and vision. The director acts as a representative for the company inside and outside the court. It is an onerous responsibility, since a director has responsibility for anything that happens within the company and under the Company Law. A director must carry out his/her duties in good faith and with full responsibility. In the event that the company suffers any losses as a result of an error or negligence on the part of a director in the course of performing his/her duty, the BoD member in question is fully and personally responsible for such losses. The law is silent on the subject of insuring the liability of a director. However, some insurance companies in Indonesia already provide directors and officers liability insurance to help directors face the future and conduct business with assurance.

6 ACCOUNTING TREATMENT

[378] The accounting standards in Indonesia refer to the Indonesian Financial Accounting Standards (IFAS or PSAK) which represent guidance issued by the Indonesian Institute of Accountants Standard Board (DSAK IAI) and the Indonesian Institute of Accountants Sharia Standard Board (DSAS IAI) as well as capital market regulatory regulations for entities under its supervision.

[379] Deviation from the IFAS/PSAK is possible but under very limited conditions in which the relevant regulatory framework permits such deviation to occur or, at least does not prohibit such deviation. In addition, the deviation in question must also be observed by all companies within the same industry (thus if there is one company operating within the same industry which does not deviate from the PSAK, then all other companies in the relevant industry are precluded from deviating from the PSAK). In relation to International Financial Reporting Standards (IFRS) it is known that the intended purpose of the International Accounting Standard Board (IASB) is full convergence with and adoption of the IFRS itself. This means that in due course IFRS convergence can be expected to align the PSAK with the IFRS, without any modification. However, the adoption of IFRS in Indonesia is not conducted on the basis of 'full adoption'. There are still some modifications in the PSAK which involve key differences from the IFRS. Therefore, for accounting purpose, Indonesian companies must expect IFRS to be implemented in relation to any provisions where the PSAK is already in line with the IFRS. Furthermore, Indonesian companies will soon feel the increasing effect of IFRS as Indonesian GAAP continues to adopt further provisions of IFRS.

[380] The merger and acquisition process may have different meanings, treatment, and arrangements, depending on whether transactions are viewed from an accounting or a legal perspective. For business combinations, PSAK 22 is consistent with IFRS 3 in all significant respects, except the addition of a reference to PSAK 28 (accounting for loss insurance) and PSAK 36 (accounting for life insurance). Under PSAK 22, most combinations are accounted for as acquisitions. Merger accounting is applied in only limited circumstances. Merger accounting is not allowed under IFRS; all business combinations must be treated as acquisitions. However, PSAK currently permits use of the combination-of-interests method in certain rare circumstances.

[381] In relation to fair values, according to the 2015 amended version of PSAK 68 on Fair Value Measurement, it is determined that fair value is a market-based measurement, not a specific measurement over an entity. For several assets and liabilities, market transactions or observable market information may be available. However, the fair value measurement objectives in both cases are the same, namely to estimate the consideration which would apply in the context of an orderly transaction to sell assets or to transfer liabilities between market participants on the relevant measurement date under prevailing market conditions (that being the exit price on the measurement date from the perspective of the market participant owning those assets or liabilities). When the price for identical assets or liabilities cannot be assessed, the entity measures the fair value using other assessment techniques which maximize the usage of relevant observable inputs and minimizes the usage of unobservable inputs. Because fair value is a market-based measurement, it is measured based on the same assumptions as the market participants will use when determining the price of the relevant assets and liabilities, including the same assumptions on risk. Consequently the actual intention of the entity to own an asset or to resolve/fulfil a liability becomes irrelevant when measuring fair value.

[382] In relation to the scope for provisioning, as regulated in PSAK 57 on Provisions, Contingent Liabilities and Contingent Assets, provisions should only be used for the purpose for which they were originally recognized. They should be reviewed at each balance sheet date and adjusted to reflect the current best estimate. If it is no longer probable that an outflow of resources will be required to settle an obligation, the provision should be reversed. Provisions can only be used for the costs of any proposed reorganization and/or integration of the business acquired where the relevant expenses are directly related to the intended purpose of making such provisions.

[383] If companies are required to capitalize goodwill, according to the 2015 amended version of PSAK 22 on Business Combinations goodwill is no longer able to be amortized since it is stated that entities are obliged to suspend the amortization of goodwill for book year periods starting on or after 1 January 2011. Therefore, an impairment test over goodwill must be conducted based on the 2014 revision of PSAK 48 on Asset Value Impairment. At the end of each reporting period, the entity in question must assess whether there is any indication that an asset may have undergone value impairment. If such an indication exists, the entity must estimate the recoverable amount of such asset. More specifically in relation to goodwill acquired on a business combination, regardless of whether or not there is any indication of value impairment, the entity in question must, not less than once a year at the minimum, conduct an impairment test by comparing the recorded value with the recoverable amount. In assessing whether the asset may or may not experience value impairment, the entity must consider, at a minimum, the following factors:

(a) Information from external sources:
  - Significant changes in market value.
  - Significant changes in technology, market, economy, and legal scope.
  - Changes in interest rate.

- The recorded amount of the entity's net assets exceeding its market capitalization.

(b) Information from internal sources:
- Proof of obsolescence or physical damage to the asset.
- Significant changes over usage, suspension, and useful lives of the asset.
- Internal proof which indicates that the economic performance of the asset is worse than expected.

[384] When there is an indication that there is a value impairment of an asset, the entity is required to measure the recoverable amount of such asset.

[385] According to the 2015 amended version of the PSAK 19 on Intangible Assets, in order to be or to continue to be recognized, intangible assets should be recognized if, and only if:

(a) There is a major possibility that the entity will gain future economic benefits from such asset.
(b) The anticipated sale/purchase consideration for such assets can be reliably measured.

[386] In assessing the probability of future economic benefits, the entity must use rational and accountable assumptions to the best of management's estimation under prevailing economic conditions during the useful life of such asset. In addition, an asset may be said to be identifiable/recognizable if:

(a) It could be separated, that is separated or differentiated from the entity itself and sold, moved, licensed, rented or exchanged, whether separately or jointly with any related contract, asset or identified liability, regardless of whether the entity intends in practice to do such thing.
(b) It arises from a contract or other legal rights, regardless of whether such rights are transferable or separated/separable from the entity itself or from other rights and obligations.

[387] PSAK 19 on Intangible Assets establishes that the appropriate accounting treatment for intangible assets is based on their useful lives. An Intangible asset with a limited useful life is amortized, and an intangible asset with an unlimited useful life is not. The period of amortization for intangible assets with limited useful lives should start when the asset is available for use, which is when the asset is located on the location and in a condition to become operational in accordance with the requirements of the management. Amortization should be suspended from the time when the asset is first classified as an owned asset to be sold, or is included in a pool of removable assets categorized as assets to be sold (in accordance with the 2014 amended version of PSAK 58 on Long Term Assets Which Owned to Be Sold and the Suspended Operation) or the date when recognition of such asset is suspended, whichever first occurs. For intangible assets with unlimited useful lives, PSAK 19 determines that such assets should not be amortized, and that an entity is required to test such assets for value impairment by comparing the recoverable amount with the recorded amount:

(a) every year, or
(b) at any time when there is an indication that any of the intangible assets in question are experiencing value impairment.

[388] According to PSAK 22 on Business Combinations, negative goodwill should be credited to the profit and loss account. It will be recorded on the credit side as a profit arising from a business combination.

According to PSAK 22 on Business Combinations, paragraph 53 states that acquisition-related costs are only those costs incurred by the acquiring party within the framework of the business combination. Moreover, paragraph 53 states that the acquiring party is obliged to record the acquisition-related costs as a liability for the period in which such costs have occurred or the services were received, with one exception, namely the cost of issuing bonds and equity, which are recognized in accordance with the 2015 adjusted version of PSAK 55 on Financial Instruments: Recognition and Measurement and with the 2014 adjusted version of PSAK 50 on Financial Instruments: Presentation and Disclosure. In general, acquisition costs are imposed on the profit and loss statement for the period when such costs were incurred.

[389] Regarding the determination of the effective date of an acquisition in Indonesia, this is governed by PSAK 22 on Business Combinations. The relevant provision states that the acquiring party identifies the acquisition date, which is the date when the acquiring party gains control over the acquired party. In general, the date when the acquiring party gains control over the acquired party is the date when the acquiring party, by virtue of the law, transfers the consideration, acquires the asset, and assumes the liabilities of the acquired party – which is usually the closing date. However, an acquiring party may gain control before or after the closing date. For instance, the acquisition date will precede the closing date if in a written agreement it is stated that the acquiring party will gain control over the acquired party on a date prior to the closing date. The acquiring party must consider all relevant facts, terms and conditions in determining the acquisition date.

[390] Moreover, as from the acquisition date, namely the date when control over the assets and operations of an acquired company (acquiree) is effectively transferred to the acquirer and the date on which the application of the purchase method of accounting is commenced, the acquiring company must:

(a) report any proceeds/distributions from the acquired company in its profit and loss statement; and
(b) report the assets and liabilities of the acquired company in its balance sheet as well as any goodwill arising from the acquisition.

[391] In accordance with accounting principles, an acquisition must be valued at its purchase price, which is established by the value of the cash paid and/or other assets transferred at the fair market value, plus other expenses directly attributed to the acquisition. Prevailing tax laws, however, stipulate that book values of the resulting merger or acquisition may be applied for tax purposes, subject to approval by the Directorate General of Taxation. Such approval may only be considered after all outstanding taxes of all legal entities are merged or acquired.

[392] According to PSAK 22 on Business Combinations, changes in the fair value of any contingent consideration recognized by the acquirer after the acquisition date may arise pursuant to additional information obtained by the acquirer after that date about facts and circumstances which existed at the acquisition date. Such changes may be represented by adjustments to the relevant measurement period. However, changes resulting from events after the acquisition date, such as achieving a particular profit target, achieving a certain share price, or achieving milestones in a research and development project, may not be taken into account as adjustments in the measurement period. The acquirer records any changes in the fair value of contingent consideration which cannot be recorded as adjustments in the measurement period as follows:

(a) Contingent consideration which is classified as equity is not remeasured; subsequent settlements of such consideration are recorded in equity.
(b) Other contingent benefits:
  (i) Within the scope of PSAK 55: Financial Instruments: Recognition and Measurement, these are measured at fair value at each reporting date and changes in fair value are recognized in profit or loss in accordance with PSAK 55.
  (ii) Not within the scope of PSAK 55, they are measured at fair value at each reporting date and changes in fair value are recognized in profit or loss.

7 FUTURE DEVELOPMENT

7.1 Key Recent Developments, Issues and Trends Relating To M&A Activity in Indonesia

[393] Due to the COVID-19 pandemic, the Government of Indonesia ratified and enacted Law No. 2 of 2020 on State Financial Policy and Financial System Stability for Handling COVID-19 pandemic. This is intended to provide protection for people's lives which are threatened by the COVID-19 spread, both from the aspect of threats to health and safety and the social and economic life of the community.

[394] In order to support the Financial System Stability Committee in the context of handling financial system stability issues, the OJK has certain authorities, one of which is to give written orders to financial services institutions to carry out a merger, consolidation, acquisition, integration and/or conversion. Thus OJK issued OJK Regulation No. 18/POJK.03/2020 on Written Orders for Handling Bank Issues and OJK Regulation No. 12/POJK.03/2020 on the Consolidation of

Commercial Banks in the context of the banking sector. Transaction trends relating to M&A in 2020 include substantial bank-related M&A, such as the merger plan between PT Bank BRIsyariah Tbk, PT Bank Syariah Mandiri and PT Bank BNI Syariah, where PT Bank BRIsyariah Tbk will become the surviving bank.

[395] Furthermore, fintech M&A and investment continues to flourish, with fintech companies in Indonesia evolving, and ranging from banks, insurance companies, and multi-finance companies, to other payment companies, P2P lending platforms, data analytics companies, and e-commerce platforms. Consolidation has been the theme in Fintech M&A activity with Gojek (PT Aplikasi Karya Anak Bangsa) actively expanding their payments services in the region via the acquisition of PT Gofin Karya Anak Bangsa and Moka Technology Solutions Pte. Ltd, in 2020.

[396] Also, other significant regulatory developments in 2020 having a direct impact on M&A and foreign investors' interests include:

- The President of the Republic Indonesia ratified and enacted Law No. 11 of 2020 on Job Creation, or known as the Omnibus Law on 2 November 2020. Law No. 11/2020 revises/amends/revokes 79 laws in a single legislative instrument, intending to improve the investment system in Indonesia, to attract investors and to create job opportunities. Law No. 11/2020 has enhanced the structure of business licenses by integrating them into a single business license.
- Furthermore, in February 2021, there are forty-five Government Regulations and four President Regulations which are the implementing regulations of the Omnibus Law that are issued, among others:
  (1) Government Regulation No. 5 of 2021 on Implementation of Risk-Based Business Licensing;
  (2) Government Regulation No. 6 of 2021 on the Implementation of Business Licensing in Regions;
  (3) Government Regulation No. 8 of 2021 on Authorized Capital of Companies and Registration of Establishment, Amendment and Disbursement of Companies That Meet the Criteria for Micro and Small Businesses;
  (4) Government Regulation No. 9 of 2021 on Tax Treatment to Support the Ease of Doing Business;
  (5) Government Regulation No. 10 of 2021 on Regional Tax and Retribution in the Framework of Supporting the Ease of Doing Business and Services in Region;
  (6) Government Regulation No. 17 of 2021 on the Fourth Amendment to Government Regulation No. 15 of 2005 on Toll Roads;
  (7) Government Regulation No. 18 of 2021 on Management Rights, Land Rights, Apartment Units and Land Registration;
  (8) Government Regulation No. 19 of 2021 on Implementation of Land Acquisition for Development for Public Interest;
  (9) Government Regulation No. 22 Year 2021 on Implementation of Environmental Protection and Management;

(10) Government Regulation No. 25 of 2021 on the Implementation of the Sector of Energy and Mineral Resources;
(11) Government Regulation No. 26 of 2021 on the Implementation of the Agricultural Sector;
(12) Government Regulation No. 27 of 2021 on the Implementation of the Marine and Fisheries Sector;
(13) Government Regulation No. 28 of 2021 on the Implementation of the Industrial Sector;
(14) Government Regulation No. 29 of 2021 on the Implementation of the Trade Sector;
(15) Government Regulation No. 30 of 2021 on Implementation of the Road Traffic and Transportation Sector;
(16) Government Regulation No. 31 of 2021 on the Implementation of the Shipping Sector;
(17) Government Regulation No. 32 of 2021 on the Implementation of the Aviation Sector;
(18) Government Regulation No. 33 of 2021 on the Implementation of the Railway Sector;
(19) Government Regulation No. 34 of 2021 on the Utilization of Foreign Workers;
(20) Government Regulation No. 35 of 2021 on Fixed Term Employment, Outsourcing, Working Hours and Rest Times and Termination;
(21) Government Regulation No. 36 of 2021 on Wages;
(22) Government Regulation No. 37 of 2021 on the Implementation of the Job Loss Security Program;
(23) Government Regulation No. 40 of 2021 on the Implementation of Special Economic Zones;
(24) Government Regulation No. 41 of 2021 on the Implementation of Free Trade Zones and Free Ports;
(25) Government Regulation No. 42 of 2021 on the Ease of National Strategic Projects;
(26) Government Regulation No. 44 of 2021 on Implementation of the Prohibition of Monopolistic Practices and Unfair Business Competition;
(27) Government Regulation No. 46 of 2021 on Post, Telecommunication and Broadcasting;
(28) Government Regulation No. 48 of 2021 on Third Amendment to Government Regulation No. 31 of 2013 on Implementation Regulations of Law No. 6 of 2011 on Immigration; and
(29) Presidential Regulation No. 10 of 2021 on the Investment Business Activities.

– KPPU issued implementing guidelines on merger, consolidation, or acquisitions, which came into force on 6 October 2020, in response to multiple interpretations of KPPU Regulation No. 3/2019. The guideline regulates a simplified M&A notification procedure, whereby the KPPU must complete its assessment within 14 business days. This is expected to occur and to be completed within 60 business days of clarification and research. This is a significantly shorter timeframe by comparison with the previous merger notification process which allowed a maximum of 150 business days. In addition, this guideline also regulates that KPPU will assess the acquisition/transfers of assets and of participating interests. Furthermore, foreign mergers having an impact on the Indonesian market will be notifiable.

7.2 Developments That Need to Be Anticipated Soon Which Are Likely to Affect How M&A Transactions Are Conducted in Indonesia

[397] Law No. 11/2020 provides that further regulations will be provided for in governmental or presidential regulations. The issuance of the relevant implementing regulations for Law No. 11/2020 further reviews and analyses are necessary to obtain a more detailed overview of its impact on various sectors, including the M&A sector. Especially, that the government is issue a negative investment list which is under the PR No. 10/2021 now called positive investment list in a presidential regulation, which include a list of prioritized business sectors and reserved business sectors for micro, small and medium enterprises and which will indicate those that are open for investment under certain conditions. While Law No. 11/2020 revokes articles regulating foreign investment thresholds under many industry-specific regulations, some have not yet been revoked. It is unclear whether these industry-specific regulations will still apply.

[398] Also, three other related draft bills are currently being prepared for future deliberation, namely: (1) the Draft Bill on the amendment of the Fiduciary Security (*Jaminan Fidusia*); (2) the Draft Bill on the amendment of Bankruptcy Law; and (3) Data Protection Law.

www.ingramcontent.com/pod-product-compliance
Lightning Source LLC
Chambersburg PA
CBHW071351230926
51846CB00002B/504
9789403533605